CHAISE LONGUE

BAXTER DURY

corsair

CORSAIR

First published in Great Britain in 2021 by Corsair

1 3 5 7 9 10 8 6 4 2

Copyright © 2021, Baxter Dury

The moral right of the author has been asserted.

A CIP catalogue record for this book
is available from the British Library.

ISBN: 978-1-4721-5513-9

Typeset in Optima by M Rules
Printed and bound in Great Britain by
Clays Ltd, Elcograf S.p.A.

Papers used by Corsair are from well-managed forests
and other responsible sources.

Corsair
An imprint of
Little, Brown Book Group
Carmelite House
50 Victoria Embankment
London EC4Y 0DZ

An Hachette UK Company
www.hachette.co.uk

www.littlebrown.co.uk

This book is dedicated to

Alfie Rowe, who we lost way too early
Pete Rush, The Sulphate Strangler
Charlie Charles
Mum & Dad

CONTENTS

1

LOST IN AUSTIN

Austin, Texas, 1999

Curtis was small, long-haired and mumbly. He was Texan in tone but looked more like a stoner hedge-hog. He warned me of his melancholic disposition and explained that, in the middle of a black period, the only solution was sleep.

I had arrived in Austin, Texas, wearing a designer puffer jacket and with little expectation. It was very hot and I was a slightly overweight twenty-six-year-old bloke with a broken heart and a dying father.

Geoff Travis, boss of Rough Trade Records, had given me some money on a whim after I persuaded him that I needed to go on a road trip with Curtis to write songs. This was a considerable risk as Geoff didn't know me, I didn't know Curtis and I hadn't given either of them much to show I was any good.

We hit the highway without a detailed plan. We had a tiny tent, some tinned pineapple and an enormous Buick we had just rented. The first objective was to reach the Gila mountain settlement deep into New Mexico. We were going to camp out among the wolves and write songs in the moonlight where the Indians once lived in caves.

We travelled through the endless symmetry that makes up Texas, eventually arriving in New Mexico. We stopped at a service station to pick up some supplies close to our destination. A large Mexican woman was sitting in the kiosk with little life in her eyes. She was screaming in Spanish into a CB radio as the light flickered behind her.

While Curtis bought some provisions I looked for the toilets. I navigated a series of small corridors that led to an outside area concealed from the front. Ahead of me was a tiger – a real one. Its face was squashed against the bars of a small cage

2

and its opiated eyes barely registered my presence. Another tiger lay behind it, gnawing on its own tail. The scenario felt apocalyptically remote and scary.

After a few hours we found a suitable place to camp to the side of the forest. One other camper van was parked in the clearing. It soon became obvious that Curtis didn't have much experience setting up a tent, which was disconcerting. We built a fire and cooked some vegetarian sausages, and sat enjoying the vastness of our surroundings.

The other camper fidgeted around and made us feel uneasy. The wolves howled, unsettling us even more, and a wall of cold night shattered our souls. We lay top-to-toe in the tiny tent, trying gather as much human warmth from each other as possible. By three in the morning I felt hypothermic and retreated back to the Buick. I ran the engine for heat while Curtis stubbornly continued to pretend to sleep. At four in the morning he knocked feebly on the window, barely able to open the door. He fell into the car and I covered him with a blanket. An hour later we abandoned the camping gear and drove off as the sun rose, illuminating the Gila River that ran through the middle of the mountain range.

To recover our excitement we headed towards El Paso on the Mexican border to cross into Juárez. We left behind the green, untouched expanse and found the terrifying bleakness of the border. As we queued up a customs officer warned us we were entering the most dangerous place in Mexico and we should never deviate from the main shopping street. We bought one bottle of tequila and spent three hours trying to get back.

We drove for another day past an indistinguishable desert until Curtis pulled the car over.

'Yoh, I feel mighty strange,' he said in a low Texan drawl. 'I'm gonna just reconfigure for a while, so y'all find yourself something of interest and we'll pick it up tomorrow.'

Unearthing something of interest was a difficult task as we were surrounded only by dust. We found an isolated motel on the side of an endless road. Curtis removed the pillows from both beds and put them on the floor, and then lay star-shaped, staring at the ceiling.

There's nothing like the open expanse of America to make you feel claustrophobic. I started to think about home. My ex-girlfriend was now dating my friend and, just days before I came out, my dad had

4

been told he had only a few months to live. I began to cry while standing outside the motel, staring at the ugly desert. There must have been skunks in the distance as I caught a waft of a sea of ancient urine.

We carried on travelling for another two weeks until we'd finally driven full circle and came back towards Austin to spend Thanksgiving with Curtis's very old mother and his awkward stepfather, a Republican ex-judge. His mum slopped turkey from a can like dog food, with the cranberry sauce already on top. The sound alone gave me an over-whelming sense of despair. The judge's enormous eyebrows made accusatory shapes when he disa-greed with anyone. I suddenly felt very homesick. I snuck away from the dinner table and secretly found a phone upstairs. I managed to get through to Dad, who I hadn't spoken to for a month. He sounded weak and just said, 'Come home as soon as you can.'

A few days later I took a short connecting flight from Austin back to Houston. The weather was awful and the tiny plane had to fly around an enormous storm cloud. There were several large Texan businessmen on board complaining about how dangerous it was to fly in these conditions, which contributed to my sense of unease. By the time I arrived in Houston I felt unprepared for the long flight home and what I had to face when I got there.

I found an airport bar and drank four pints to quell my nerves. I felt jubilant as I boarded the plane and spread out on a row of empty seats at the back. As the plane's engines roared in preparation for take-off, I stood up and started walking down the aisle. The plane lifted off the ground and I unsteadily made it to the middle section. The flight attendant grabbed me from behind and started shouting at me to sit down. I wriggled past her and opened up the toilet door, and then started pissing inside my trousers, at which point she let go of me. I was then told that I would be cautioned for violating aviation law and was made to sit at the front of the plane in my wet trousers. A few hours later I was woken up by someone politely tapping my shoulder. She said she was English and that her and her friend thought I was hilarious but I'd been snoring so loudly that the rest of the plane hated me.

*

I got back in time to help look after Dad for the last few months of his life, which was as uplifting as it was sad as he slowly faded. His last performance was at the Palladium Theatre in the West End, where he was wheeled on in a box trolley pushed by his best friend Derek The Draw (Derek Hussey). Dad was jaundiced and impossibly thin, and he could hardly talk let alone sing, but he did.

After another month in hospital he opted to come back home to die. My stepmother Sophy, my sister Jemima, my two younger half-brothers Bill and Albert and I did what we could to make him feel as comfortable as possible. Dad mustered all his strength to boss us around until one day, on 27 March 2000, he lay down, sort of smiled and grimaced at the same time, and then went. He was fifty-seven.

On the day of his funeral, a procession led by two police outriders and a horse-drawn hearse covered in floral tributes went from Hampstead to Golders Green Crematorium. Durex, Dad's nickname, was written in white lilies down one side of the ornate Victorian carriage, which summed everything up perfectly. The wake was at the Forum in Kentish Town. This was the first time I ever performed on stage, singing a song called 'My Old Man' written

by Dad about his own father, which was both frightening and beautiful.

My relationship with Dad was a good one considering how complicated he could be. And maybe
I tried over the years to feel sorry about some of
the craziness that was bestowed upon my life as a
child but now I feel differently about that and more
understanding. What made me start writing down
my memories wasn't because I wanted to reveal all
about my famous dad or my incredible mum, who
both contributed to my happiness and sometimes
instability. I'm more interested in the viewpoint I
had watching some of the events unravel. I've tried
to explain those events in the only way I can, which
is at times chaotic but I never really went to school
so this is a personal triumph of applied effort. I jump
back and forth in time as it feels natural to explain
my past like this. My older years, being clearer,
hold memories I still occupy; the younger years
are foggier and the stories are sometimes based on
folklore and a little research. I have tried to build a
sense of my childhood, not a detailed account of
factual events.

Chiswick, London, 1984

Mr Boil taught graphics and design. He was fully aware that this subject had no function to anyone and was mostly an exercise in morale breaking. But that premise is exactly what excited Mr Boil. He was a broad-shouldered man with a military bearing, a frightening moustache and a fixed expression of contempt. He hated the children and enjoyed the fact that the children hated him.

He broke the class up into controllable groups based on their disruptive potential. Jamie and I were considered agitators so we were placed at the front of the class among some more stable workers. Jamie was a volatile and an unwanted ally most of the time but we found common interest in how much we disliked this lesson. The fact Mr Boil was like a coiled spring made the sport of irritating him a bonus. He generated an unpleasant energy that smothered his own judgement and made his responses irrational. No one dared ask him anything as he stood with his back to the class drawing unknown symbols on to his blackboard.

Jamie began the ceremony of undoing Mr Boil's concentration by producing strange noises that sounded like mating cries. He threw his 'ooooooaaagh' sounds into the class like a veteran ventriloquist. Mr Boil's head spun round, unable to place the origins of the noise. As soon as he resumed his position facing the blackboard I emulated Jamie's effort as best I could but with more intensity: 'AAAAAAOOOOOGH.' Mr Boil now turned his entire body round to face the class, his neck muscles pulsating with tension. He walked towards us with his hairy nostrils contracting as though he could smell the insurgent. He stared at me directly in the eyes and made a firm statement to the class. 'I will not in any way accept any more SHIT from any of you, just see.'

It was a clear point of intention and just where we wanted him.

At the desk between Jamie and me was a frail young boy called Elliot Smould. His delicate hands were always nervously rearranging his desk contents into different symmetrical patterns. His huge mane of black hair clothed the strange-shaped head that housed his enormous brain.

Jamie whispered, 'Elliot, you speck, make a fucking noise.'

Elliot pretended not to hear. His eyes widened,

hoping to attract the attention of Mr Boil, who was once again drawing angry rectangular designs on his blackboard. Jamie repeated the command with the added threat of violence, 'I'll fucking knock you, you cunt. Do it.'

Elliot, petrified and in an impossible situation, weighed up the risk of angering Mr Boil, who as a teacher would have some measure of self-control, against being punished by Jamie, who enjoyed other people's suffering.

Elliot's skeletal body began to shake as he drew in a large breath and prepared himself for the sacrifice. He then let out everything he had in him as though it was his final statement to the world. 'OOOOOOOOOOOAAAAAEEGH,' he shrieked tearfully.

Without hesitation Mr Boil pivoted round and instinctively threw the wooden chalk eraser at Elliot's head, his enormous cranium being difficult to miss. It bounced off his forehead, just above his thick-rimmed glasses, and both Jamie and I were showered with blood. He fell backwards off his chair, crashed to the floor and lay there stunned. Mr Boil, now fully engaged, marched towards the motionless Elliot, grabbed him by the legs and dragged him out of the classroom. In the doorway we saw Elliot being forcibly stood up while Mr Boil held him by his neck and then escorted off for sentencing.

We erupted in laughter as this was beyond all of our expectations. It was a beautifully choreographed act of cruelty at the expense of Elliot. Violence was an infectious cycle as long as you could divert the attention away from yourself: anyone else was worth sacrificing in pursuit of a pain-free life. But I did feel awful for poor Elliot and I think he knew that. Not that it ever helped.

When I arrived at Chiswick School my view of the larger world was still unformed as I had been living in Tring, a small, claustrophobic town on the borders of Hertfordshire, for the previous five years. I had bad hair and rural clothes.

The school itself was geographically snug, placed in between Chiswick House, a neo-Palladian villa with a large park, and the River Thames. Chiswick itself represented the idea of middle-class comfort. It had a provincial sleepiness to it but the school had another reality. The wealthier children were sent out to the local private schools. Chiswick School was for the deprived kids. Our family had some money but were still tethered to socialist ideas of fair schooling. Or, rather, Dad had a strong policy of selective spending.

My class had a disproportionate amount of fucked-up kids in it but three really stood out. Lee, Jamie and Patrick were all sadistic. I suffered immensely at the hands of these three until I found ways of reversing their viciousness.

Everyone knew that I had a famous dad and reacted to it in different ways but some resented it. They viewed me as an outsider and I was. It wasn't because we were wealthy as we weren't rich. I was just different in the way I looked and spoke: I was bohemian and odd. We did live in a nice mansion flat that we bought from the proceeds of selling our equally nice house in Tring. Clive, Mum's partner, worked in a picture-framing shop and Mum lived off the small allowance Dad gave her for the upkeep of me and Jemima. Mum and Dad had split up quite soon after I was born in 1971 but had remained very close and now we lived just a few miles down the river from him.

Lee singled me out straight away. He sat behind me and whispered threatening comments. The moment I answered back he picked me up and slammed me down on my own desk. His face was already formed into that of an older person. His hair and uniform were always immaculate as a point of pride. Something or someone had robbed him of all of his empathy, and I was everything he didn't understand and wanted to destroy.

A month later Jamie broke my nose as he disliked how comfortable I was becoming within the group of classmates. He landed his forehead on the bridge of it without warning. Blood splattered across the corridor outside the classroom. The suddenness of his actions and the deeper level of violence weren't something I was prepared for. The lack of concern from the teachers was also a shock. I was given a detention for being late after cleaning up the blood.

Then there was Patrick, the ultimate pathological kid. There were no limits to his brutality but, unlike the others, he was approachable and often funny.

Most days we would find ourselves unsupervised and roaming the streets of Chiswick because of the teachers' strikes. We became more and more of a nuisance to the local businesses as we tried to find ways to entertain ourselves. We would steal anything, break anything. We smashed all the ornate windows in the seventeenth-century house in Chiswick Park.

Patrick and Lee had stolen a motorbike and were casually trying to kickstart it in the street opposite the school. While I was walking past them during the lunch break, Patrick ushered me over to inspect the rusty carcass and honoured me with the chance of helping him make it work. This meant pushing it from the side while he sat pulling the throttle.

Amazingly it spluttered into action and he sped off down the small street. He came back round and offered me the next turn. The significance of being chosen above Lee was a breakthrough in my acceptance. He was offering me friendship while also putting my life in danger.

At that moment, we were surrounded by angry shop owners horrified by what we were doing. The engine stalled and I dismounted the bike, and nonchalantly walked back past them into the school.

In the following months Patrick displayed great affection towards me and we would awkwardly hang out after school. I knew this was an unsafe friend to have as he was plainly disturbed but I didn't have much choice.

One opportune afternoon I decided to take

Patrick along the river to where Dad lived in Hammersmith. I calculated that meeting Dad might make an impression on him that would lessen the chances of him eventually turning on me, which I had guessed were guaranteed at some point.

Structurally, Dad's flat was impressive with a sixty-foot balcony overlooking the Thames. Internally, it was a shithole. It had a damp, bohemian man odour to it. Dad's girlfriend at the time, Anthea Cocktail, had made lots of cheap beaded curtains that cascaded down as you entered. She was named after a Brompton cocktail, a form of euthanasia (vodka, heroin, cocaine) popular in 1920s old people's homes. She liked to throw furniture, and on a few occasions herself, into the river after an argument.

The front room had one broken antique chair and a rotting chaise longue. The television was on top of an old dessert trolley and a huge Union Jack, which some sailors had stripped from HMS *Belfast* as a gift, covered the main wall.

Dad was sitting with the Sulphate Strangler, a six-foot-seven malodorous giant, on his church pew on the balcony.

This was the first time they had seen each other since Strangler was rumoured to have smuggled guns in a bass drum while touring America. They were drunk in the sun, both with their tops off. Several beer cans were discarded around their feet.

Patrick was wary as Strangler stood up to greet us, his enormous body dripping in sweat.

'Strangler, is it?' I asked shyly.

'Pete,' said Strangler firmly.

Dad made no effort at all and continued staring at the blazing river.

'Dad, Pete, this is Patrick.'

Strangler just glared at me with his head tipping from side to side, his earrings making a pretty sound.

Dad made a sheep noise without looking at us. Patrick stuttered.

'What did you say?' Strangler demanded.

Patrick said nothing. Dad just looked at the river and made more sheep noises. Strangler sat back down on the fragile pew, resuming his sunbathing position.

Dad's head finally turned towards Patrick and he said, 'Do you like sheep, Patrick?' Dad took an enormous drag on his joint and blew out the smoke provocatively.

Patrick edged backwards and grabbed my arm for

assurance. 'Ha ... fuck ... what?' is all he managed. Dad and Strangler maintained their indifference.

'We've been let off school so I thought I'd come and say hello.'

There was no response from either of them.

I guided Patrick away from the balcony and apologised for how weird they were being but Patrick pretended not to be bothered. We walked back to school in silence.

After that Patrick's interest in me faded and I was left alone. I imagine it had something to do with how bonkers it was at Dad's that day, as even I was a little shocked. But it didn't change the way Patrick was to others.

2

FAMILY

By the time my older sister Jemima, Mum, her partner Clive and I all moved to Chiswick I was old enough to want diversity and poetic opportunities. Not glue sniffing with Carnage on a disused climbing frame, as was the reality in Tring. Carnage had dwarfism but compensated by being extremely violent to anyone that dared suggest he was any different. I found this out on the first day of Tring secondary school when he used a chair to stand on and then headbutted me. Tring wasn't poor but just deprived of culture and hope.

In many ways, it was the most frightening place I have ever lived.

I was always restless in Tring. I was first arrested when I was only ten after I persuaded my friend Caspian to help collect cowpats in an old frying pan we had stolen from my kitchen. We waited on the top of a footbridge overlooking the A41, a small stretch of motorway connecting Berkhamsted with Aylesbury. I flung the shit at the first vehicle I saw travelling at speed. The car skilfully manoeuvred, preventing any of the matter landing directly on the windscreen, but it then skidded sharply from one lane to another and then rolled on to the bank. We both ran without any consideration for the driver, went down the other side of the bridge and sprinted along a country lane. Unbelievably the driver leapt out of his car and jumped over a gigantic fence. Caspian, being faster, disappeared ahead but I was quickly grabbed from behind and pushed to the ground.

'POLICE!'

Improbably, I had thrown cow shit at the only off-duty policeman driving at that moment under the bridge.

He screamed at my friend to stop with such

authority that Caspian froze in the moment. We both stood traumatised and whimpering. He asked whose idea it was to throw shit at a moving car and who owned the frying pan. After realising that Caspian was less involved, he aimed his long speech mostly at me but decided that neither of us were a threat to society and let us go.

We cried all the way home and made a pact not to tell our parents. Caspian immediately told my mum who in turn told his. I was gently reprimanded and he was scolded into a pulp.

A week later, Caspian and I burnt our eyelashes off on the gas stove trying to light cigarettes we had stolen from my sister.

By the time we moved to Chiswick, Jemima and I had grown accustomed to Clive being around and that was OK. Just. But we had spent the majority of our childhoods without somebody influencing our mum. We were free spirited in the best tradition of children brought up within a single-parent family, and who at times may have had too much choice. Clive definitely had his work cut out for him. But Mum saw something in him that was reassuringly different. He was smart, handsome and a little tense. Mum needed someone like Clive to sober up some of the mania of Dad's success. They had met while on an etching course where Clive had impressed Mum with his shading skills and general Welshness.

Dad's girlfriend Anthea, on the other hand, was equal victim and propagator of unnecessarily awkward moments. She was a lot younger than Dad but socially ambitious and wanted to be close to someone that had status. She was part of an avant-garde knitting scene which made clothes for Hyper Hyper and was associated with bands like Sigue Sigue Sputnik. Dad grew his hair long and dyed it black, and wore grotesque knitted cardigans created by her. They thrived for a while on a negative energy at the expense of everyone around them. She was a conditioned flirt and would rest on the knee of anyone likely to cause offence, as she had originally done with Dad to capture his attention. Their incendiary spirit wasn't always sensitive to Jemima and me. Her interest in us was only ever meant to frustrate Dad. Mostly we were an inconvenience to her. But he wasn't any better.

One afternoon not long after we'd moved to

London Dad rang Mum from a pay phone in a panic saying he'd been beaten up and that he'd escaped from the Hammersmith flat. Jemima, Mum and I went to investigate and found Dad hiding around the corner with blood pouring from his eye. While Mum and Jemima took Dad back to Chiswick, I had the unpleasant task of going into the flat to try to collect his belongings. Each wall had been daubed in red lipstick with different angry statements. 'Cocaine, black leather whips, kinky Ian Dury' was written over the mirrors in the bathroom. I retrieved his toothbrush and quickly retreated from the room, uncertain if Anthea was lurking in the bedroom.

Chairs were overturned, coffee was over the ceiling. I could hear the faint sound of bleeping from the front balcony. The handsfree telephone was bobbing up and down in the river. Anthea had smashed it around Dad's head before throwing it into the Thames. It made one last bleep before submerging.

As I was about to leave I noticed that, in the bedroom next to the entrance, the small balcony door above the street was open. As I peered over the balcony, I could see that a kitchen chair had been thrown through the soft roof of a convertible Golf directly below.

Mum is difficult to describe but the best people always are. Compared to Dad, she was less obvious and she didn't require the level of attention he did. There's a loss of boundaries when your parent needs you to be their audience, as Dad did. He broke your confidence and replaced it with his own. Mum listened and supported, and was always around.

Mum, who was christened Elizabeth and known as Betty, was quietly self-assured as she knew from a very young age that she was very good at art. She was the youngest of three sisters who grew up outside Newport, South Wales. Both of her parents were artists: her father Thomas Rathmell was a figurative painter, and was the head of Newport School of Art, and her mother Lillian was a textile artist. After meeting in Liverpool they moved to Caerleon, Gwent, where Thom established himself as a painter and was honoured by commissions to capture Charles's investiture as the Prince of Wales in 1969 and to paint the Welsh rugby team. Thomas was a quiet, complex man and a repeat philanderer. He would commonly go missing for months at a time with one of his students. On one occasion when Mum was a toddler she saw her father pushing his latest 'arrangement' on the swings in the local park and was ushered away by Lillian so as not to inconvenience him. But Thomas doted on Mum and she was the only one of the three daughters to pursue art.

She graduated from Newport School of Art and went to the Royal College of Art in London to complete her MA in 1963. She dated a group of unwashed men before ending up with Dad in 1966. They both graduated after being taught by Peter Blake. They shared a flat together in Chiswick during which time they had Jemima and got married. Dad was outspoken and gregarious, and he found some work doing illustrations for the *Sunday Times* and other publications, but Mum was less willing to play that game.

My paternal granny lived in Hampstead in a beautiful flat with a huge garden on Fitzjohn's Avenue. It was bought with the first evidence of Dad's success.

Her knee-length silver hair was always neatly rolled up into two buns like a Soviet housewife; to me she was the portrait of a perfect granny. She had hundreds of antique inkwells lined up on shelves that overlooked the front bay windows and created a kaleidoscope of colourful light when the sun shone through them, which I found mesmerising. The garden had shrubs, bushes, oak trees, and many different plants and flowers that were roughly landscaped, making it seem endless and secretive. At the back stood a tropical greenhouse with rare species of cacti that seemed otherworldly. It was a wild and magical place and always felt like a hidden sanctuary when I was a child.

She was the middle daughter raised in Mevagissey, a pretty coastal village in Cornwall. My great-grandfather John Cuthbertson Walker was the local doctor. Originally from Donegal in Ireland, the Presbyterian Walker family were well-established dairy farmers, but one hundred and fifty years before, an illicit marriage between a Catholic farm boy and one of the young Walker women had caused a curse to be placed on the female line of the family. None of the female Walkers married or had children, until Peggy, my granny, broke the curse by marrying an

East End bus driver (strictly speaking, he was from Southborough in Kent) named Bill Dury.

I never met my paternal grandfather but he was a mythologically important figure. There is a small chance he was descended from a long line of Kentish smugglers called the Hawkhurst Gang who terrorised the south-east of England in the 1700s but that's unproven. In the many photos I've seen of him, Bill looked like a handsome potato and was always beautifully dressed. He had aspirations of becoming a boxer at a young age but instead was forced to leave school at thirteen when his father became too ill to support the family. After a few years of menial work he eventually joined a coach company and was taught how to drive. He worked on the London buses until after the war, at which point he got his chauffeur's licence. He then drove a Bentley for various rich families and film stars like Danny Kaye.

He met my granny in a pub in north London in the early 1930s. Bill was obsessed by his own class elevation and Peggy desperately wanted a baby in view of the Walker curse. They dated for a few years and, at the onset of the Second World War, quickly got married. Both families struggled with the awkward class divide. The Durys were intimidated by the bohemian intelligentsia who the Walker women represented. Bill had difficulty competing with the three sisters' interests in world politics, literature and Middle Eastern philosophy.

Bill was occupationally exempt from conscription in the war and moved Peggy to a safer house on the outskirts of Harrow. After a year, she fell pregnant with Dad and gave birth to him on 12 May 1942. When the Blitz extended to the suburbs of London she took Dad with her to Cornwall to stay with her mother. Bill remained in London to continue driving the buses and they never got back together, to his disappointment.

All three sisters were highly educated, Granny being the only one to drop out of university in favour of becoming a midwife. Aunt Elizabeth, the eldest, followed the family tradition and became a doctor and Aunt Moll worked for the education board.

Aunt Moll, to me, looked and acted vaguely like Yoda from *Star Wars*. She had perfectly white hair that was cropped at the fringe. She lived in a very old thatched cottage among the few that made up the tiny village of Oving in Buckinghamshire. She shared the house with three other women, Hill, Nora and Mim, who like Aunt Moll had no discernible interest in men but were not outwardly gay either. They were from a generation that decided not to question the consequences of their sexuality. They each had their own appointed chair that faced towards an old log fire and would ruminate for most of the day like a council of wise witches. They were connected by their spiritual and philosophical belief in Basanta Kumar Mallik, a metaphysical ecologist from Delhi. His teachings were concerned about the world's industrial crisis way before the modern infatuation. Aunt Moll co-edited *Ecology, Culture and Philosophy*, a collection of his essays on the environment, and spent a lot of time in India. On the one occasion she managed to meet my baby son Kosmo, just before she died, she picked him up, held him to the light and said, '*She's* a lovely boy, lead the way he will,' just like Yoda.

Peggy, my granny, was also progressive and proactive, and after we moved back to London I would regularly visit her, either with Dad or on my own. Granny would involve herself in our lives usually to our benefit and sometimes she would exceed what you would expect from someone in their eighties. For instance, she took an active interest in my graffiti, which I was obsessed with at the time, and would politely ask me for details about it. She knew it involved a level of criminality but that didn't seem to bother her.

While watching *TV-AM*, a hugely popular break-fast show in the 1980s, she saw that Brim Fuentes, a Bronx-based graffiti artist, was due on the following day to talk about how graffiti art was transitioning from the street to trendy galleries. She contacted the station and said she wanted to meet Brim with her thirteen-year-old grandson. And that's exactly what occurred. It was a bewilderingly surreal moment.

Brim was polite and obliging and he and Granny immediately bonded. I just remained silent. 'It's very nice to meet you, Mrs Peggy – you a very beauti-ful English lady – and you Dexter. This has been a fucked up thang being here and I'm real grateful.'

'Quite wonderful, I'm sure,' said Granny.

Granny asked him a series of questions related to his upbringing in what we only knew as a distant and scary place. He spoke for an hour about race, crime and art.

'We all just climbing over shit to make art, Mrs Peggy, and those motherfuckers, pardon me, without much foresight are closing that down without considering any benefits. This shit is pure and we're not breaking anything that matters, no windows, we're just bringing colour and hope.'

Granny stared intently at Brim and simply said, 'I wonder how we move on.'

He talked about his Puerto Rican family and the hardships of growing up in a racially divided and bankrupt city, as New York was in the mid-eighties.

'Y'all a fine lady, Mrs Peggy, and I really appreciate you listening to all this,' he said with genuine feeling. I had been completely forgotten about by then as my silence made me invisible.

When my attendance at Chiswick School started to falter it was Granny that suggested that I try King Alfred's for a trial to see if its unique teaching methods might capture my imagination. Tony, the head of English, lived above her in Fitzjohn's Avenue and they had become good friends so it was easily arranged.

The school was beautifully located on the north end of Hampstead Heath. There was no uniform, everyone seemed to smile like a Stepford wife, and a goat was tied to a pole in the middle of the uneven football pitch. The teachers had quaint names like

Bob and Samantha and some were expressive in the way they dressed. One wore the outfit of a town crier without any reason or embarrassment. I was gently herded around from class to class with little explanation of what was expected. The lessons had no clear separation of subject and it felt like one long free period. The other kids were precociously talkative and didn't seem to have much concern about what the teachers thought. I slowly assumed that I could do what I wanted, so gradually became louder and braver. Eventually, on the third day, while in what nominally seemed to be a maths lesson, I threw four chairs out of the window to see what the reaction would be. Suddenly I discovered where the boundaries lay. The smiling stopped and I was escorted to what seemed like a therapy session, similar to what I would later experience at Great Ormond Street Hospital. They spoke to me kindly and slowly, and said they understood what I was trying to achieve but maybe this school wasn't the place for someone like me right now. In hindsight I wish I had stayed there as that school was in fact designed for someone like me, but I just didn't understand that at the time and pushed them too far.

3

FRIENDS

The Gallagher family lived on Irvine Road, Shepherd's Bush, in a large squat close to Hammersmith. Micky played the keyboards in Dad's band, the Blockheads, and his two sons Luke and Ben were the only kids I knew my age in London when I arrived. Whereas only one of my parents smoked pot and was unlikely to get out of bed before midday, they had two. The house was divided between the adults and children, and the basement was dedicated to expressiveness and was full of instruments and games. Both Luke and

Ben as a result were exceptionally good at everything creative. We had a shared interest in hip hop, breakdancing and, mostly, graffiti as it was slowly filtering through from America in the early eighties. Luke was brilliant at it, which I exploited. I would pass his art off as mine at my school. This seemed to soften some of the aggression I was experiencing at the time. Luke must have understood that this was what I was doing but decided not to say anything.

As a teenager Micky had considered joining the clergy, as was the expectation of his religious family. But a few years later, in 1965, at only twenty years old he replaced Alan Price on the keyboards in the Animals. They were at the height of their fame with 'The House of the Rising Sun' being a hit across the world. He subsequently left his home town of Newcastle and toured across America and never looked back. He had a strong sense of his Catholic roots but with a new open-minded outlook that the sixties and being in a rock 'n' roll band inspired.

The Gallagher house was free of normal rules and had a spontaneous energy to it. When Luke, Ben and I decided that we should try and spray our ideas on a public wall it was Aileen, their mother, that encouraged it. She woke us up at 3 a.m., made us some toast and gave us calming drops from her cabinet of potions. The designated wall was on the side of the Hammersmith & West London College that had relative cover away from the main road. Luke's steely nerve kept him focused and he and Ben managed to complete most of the design. I panicked and ran back and forth from one end of the street to the other, convinced of our imminent capture. Luke and I were only thirteen and Ben just eleven.

Soon after, Ben and I smoked our first joint together after stealing hash from his parents. We broke into a disused railway building to the side of Olympia station, placed the whole lump into a Rizla and sprinkled it with a tiny bit of tobacco. We waited for any great revelation as to why most adults we knew smoked hash but nothing very special happened. From that point on we persevered, easily taking it from either parent's stash box until they realised and we had to start looking elsewhere.

At the time, the All Saints Road in Ladbroke Grove was west London's drug-dealing front line, mostly run by Jamaicans. Different types of hash could be purchased in a variety of sizes, the smallest being a £5 draw. This could be a stick of Red Leb, a lump of Moroccan rocky or more commonly a bit of plastic dustbin lid. Ben and I would nominate one of us to brave the scary line of dealers to find someone willing to sell to us. As soon as we scored we would run as fast as we could as we were trespassing into an unfriendly grown-up world. Sometimes the area could feel dangerous as there was so much tension between the police and the local community. Once, in the middle of the Notting Hill Carnival, Ladbroke Grove seemed more volatile than usual so Ben and I took cover at Joe Strummer's house off the All Saints on Lancaster Road. His house was several floors of sprawling chaos full of every weirdo to be found locally. Micky had worked for the Clash over the years and was a regular member of the touring band so Ben had close ties to Joe's family.

We scurried through a mesh of drunk adults towards the roof where Ben knew of a secret place where we could smoke our hash undisturbed. We climbed a precarious ladder from the attic and sat with our legs dangling over Joe's roof and rolled our joint. Surveying the festivities, we could see across the whole of west London. We drank a beer and flicked tiny bits of slate at the revellers many storeys below. Then we both decided we needed to piss but were too stoned to make the arduous journey back down. We stood up on the precarious ledge and urinated off the side in unison. We then began the slow descent down the many flights of stairs where we were confronted by Joe and Micky. They were drenched in what I could only assume was piss and looked very angry. They asked us where we'd been and we answered simultaneously, denying we'd been near the roof, and without hesitating ran past them and out of the front door. This was the only occasion I ever met Joe.

Luke and Ben may have felt that I leaned on them a little more for friendship than they did on me. Maybe some of Micky's frustrations with the music business played out between us. Dad was a difficult person to work for and Micky would find himself in the uncomfortable position of being a mediator between the management and an underpaid band.

Halfway through a concert at the Hammersmith Odeon, Dad drunkenly started to forget his lyrics in the middle of 'Reason to be Cheerful' and began to shout 'Fucking breakdance' instead. It was the first televised concert to be shown on the then new TV station Channel 4.

Ray, his then minder, was ushered over from the side of the stage and Dad told him to find us. Luke, Ben and I were found pillaging the dressing room of all its food and booze, and were told to get on stage immediately. Luke and Ben, as expected, calmly accepted that this would be a fun challenge but I was less assured. Luke was on first and confidently walked to the centre of the stage while Dad, still drunkenly hunched over his microphone, continually shouted 'breakdance'. Luke shifted from side to side in what was known as uprock and then dived on to the floor, spun round on his head and finished off with a perfect windmill. Ben wormed along the floor and then spun round on his hand and landed back on his feet triumphantly. I came on, slightly portly, and tripped over my first piece of legwork. I awkwardly transitioned into a failed backspin, which delivered me on to my knees. Dad, without considering the effect of our surnames, announced us all individually as we stood in a line. Luke and Ben both received a warm cheer but the audience erupted when my name was announced.

*

After adapting to life at Chiswick School and taming some of the threats I was then faced with the boredom of it. I wasn't able to be a part of the system for very long and found many different ways to avoid it until I became brave enough to accept that the consequences of not going didn't outweigh going.

I had an old letter from my mum that I used as a forger's alphabet. I applied tracing paper and would carefully reprint her handwriting to suit whatever excuse I needed. I was an accomplished thief so could steal food and then creep on to the roof of my mum's flat and sit there all day just smoking pot. Then I'd sneak back into the flat when it was free for a moment of warmth. If I was lucky, I would have someone to truant with as they potentially would have an empty home during the day.

While bunking off school I was caught stealing a pair of sunglasses in Boots on Kensington High Street. My friend had managed to wriggle away from the two female store detectives before I was held tightly on either side in the foyer of the tube station among a crowd of busy commuters. The police arrived and I was taken to a damp, dark cell in the bottom of Notting Hill police station. They removed my shoelaces and examined my clothes, where they found the remnants of my week's haul. Toxic silver pens, perfumed rubbers and other pointless stationery popular at the time were concealed in the inner lining of my jacket. My simple crime was now elevated to something more serious but no one could be contacted at home so I was left alone to consider my actions. The police were more interested in my famous dad and were baffled as to why I was stealing cheap sunglasses.

A kindly CID detective sat with me in my cell and showed me pictures of her cats playing in the garden. She must have felt sorry for me, which softened the outcome as they eventually let me go without much fuss. Mum received a letter a few days later but it had less of an impact after the event. The routine of bunking off school and being caught by the police became something everyone expected and there was less of a reaction each time. To live as a truant is to live without any of your normal entitlements as you're a day ghost and your greatest challenge is boredom.

Mum tried to understand why I wasn't happy at school and sent me to an educational psychologist at Great Ormond Street Hospital. I was given some blurred images to respond to and told to be honest about how I felt. They said I had a slow learning capacity and no obvious solution was prescribed.

Mum would drive me through the school gates to ensure I entered the building. I would sprint through the main corridor into the playground, then back through the dining hall and out of a small door used by the kitchen staff. A hole in the perimeter fence was just big enough for me to squeeze through and I was back on to the streets.

I'm not sure why I hated school so much. Dad's fame brought a lot of attention and I was relatively shy. I would either try and disappear or fight back if there was any negativity. By the time we had arrived in Tring, Dad was very well known. Bishop Wood Junior School was small and, at times, my presence unleashed a torrent of abuse from the older kids, which I mostly learned to ignore. A few times I was pinned to the ground as they shouted lyrics from one of Dad's songs and called him a spastic. But then I retaliated and smashed a few of them in the head, which made me feel better. When I got to Chiswick, this became less possible.

4

BOYHOOD IN BUCKINGHAMSHIRE

Aylesbury, 1974–9

Even from an early age I found it difficult being at school. Before Tring and before we had any real money, Mum, Jemima and I moved to Aylesbury when I was around four. It was more rundown than all the subsequent areas we would live in but I had a great attachment to it.

Mount Pleasant was a predominantly Pakistani community but there were Italians, Moroccans and

Jamaicans as well. Amjid and Ajmal Sadiq were my best friends and they lived next door. They had been renamed Colin and James to anglicise them for people like us. Their dad was a quiet, brooding man whose temper was always barely concealed. The walls were thin between the houses and everything could be heard. We were the odd ones out, as we would always continue to be in every street in which we lived.

We lived in a cosy, semi-detached house full of orange and brown octagon shapes that coloured the walls and curtains, and it had a tiny garden. My first memory is of setting light to one of Mum's paintings or maybe it was a cushion. I can't really remember but I do recall lighting a match and placing it under something and watching it burn. I stood for maybe a minute admiring the flames and then walked back into the front room to watch TV. I heard Mum run down the stairs and scream. The house started to fill with smoke as we evacuated into the street, and Mum went to the neighbour's house to call 999. The fire engine arrived in time to prevent the front room disappearing in flames but a canal of ash-stained water ran from the house into the drain outside. The room was scorched and blackened but still intact.

I'm not sure why I did it or if Mum reprimanded me afterwards. I think she must have been distracted all the time at that stage and I was looking for attention. But I don't remember her ever shouting much. Mum had been on her own for a few years with two children by then and we had no money so it must have been tough.

Mrs Sadiq would stare at the unwashed display of bruises and soiled purple flares that I was, and try and feed and wash me at any given opportunity. I would long to be at the Sadiqs' house permanently and found the people and cramped conditions reassuring, whereas our house had the haunted feeling of a broken home.

Their father was sometimes temperamental and to me he seemed a little brutal, but maybe that's just because Jemima and I didn't have a dad around. Mrs Sadiq displayed the obedience that was expected of her but in truth quietly managed the home and everyone in it. I commonly slept underneath Colin and James's bunk beds on some cheap nylon pillows. We would ogle at the lingerie section in the ubiquitous clothing catalogues. Colin would teach me swear words in Urdu that if repeated in earshot of Mr Sadiq would ensure that one of the boys would feel the belt, but I was out of bounds.

We weaved in and out of a patchwork of allotments that extended from one end of the street, and would climb a tree that seemed to tickle the sky. James had no logical calculation of fear and would attempt ridiculous stunts to impress us. After he fell, he wouldn't have any concern for the bone protruding from his arm. His dad would lightly beat him for the embarrassment, and then we would walk him to the hospital.

I would exploit James's willingness to please and lead him into any trouble I could find. Colin was older and protective of him, and guided him away from my influence knowing the consequences of being naughty were dealt with harshly in their family whereas my mum didn't have much discipline in her range of parenting.

Rafael lived opposite with just his mother. She would stand at her front porch screaming at him in anxious Neapolitan. Rafael would sheepishly return to his house and be placed under strict orders not to play with us. She permanently monitored the street, trying to regulate her son's exposure to a world she had not chosen for him.

Rafael was compensated with whatever he wanted and the house was stocked with shiny objects no one else had like a Betamax video player (this was the precursor to a VHS video player and was twice the size). When she left him alone the Sadiq boys and I would raid his house to enjoy the spoils with which he'd recently been indulged. We found a stash of Italian porn films that must have belonged to her. We sat and tentatively watched each one, transfixed by the unexplained actions and pretending to understand what was going on, but were really frightened by the grotesque soup of bodies. We gulped down a bottle of amaretto, James taking the majority in one swig. He collapsed on the floor, his body convulsing while a foamy puddle of spittle appeared at the side of his mouth. Colin, knowing he had to do something to save his brother's life, faced the impossible task of telling his father. After James returned from the hospital, his dad beat him once again for the embarrassment.

Colin, James and I were inseparable. Our main theme was to avoid Fontaine Carter, a large Jamaican kid who bullied us all. I made things worse by trying to convince Fontaine to eat a sandwich made from our shit, or maybe it was just mine. I had a tendency to invite the other two into commotions that Colin would have to solve. He was older, stronger and precociously mature.

But the incident with the sandwich, even though never consumed, culminated in a street battle involving all of us bearing sticks. Fontaine Carter had the majority of local kids on his side and it felt like it was just Colin, James and I versus the rest of the neighbourhood. I had the largest stick and Colin wrapped cloth around his fists to improve his punch, as seen in martial arts films. Rafael's mum, in a rare celebratory moment, came out to applaud what she thought was a game. My mum followed with her Rolleiflex camera, which she used to capture moments of real life for her paintings. Other parents came out to encourage what looked like simple fun. No one got hurt, and Fontaine Carter remained top dog.

Aylesbury was by no means a spectacular home but it was ours. Jemima and I both had rooms and Mum had a studio in the garage.

Wingrave, 1971, and the Split

On 18 December 1971 I was born in an old vicarage in the small village of Wingrave in Buckinghamshire while Dad was rehearsing with his band Kilburn and the High Roads in the basement below. Their rendition of 'Johnny B. Goode' was the first music I heard before my exhausted mum effectively told them to shut the fuck up. Dad came to say hello and nearly dropped me in his excitement, and then went back to tell the band I was a boy and continue rehearsing.

Wingrave was a beautifully decrepit house with many rooms and a sprawling, overgrown garden. Aunt Moll had found it close to her village when Mum and Dad could no longer afford to live in Chiswick after having my sister in the late sixties. It was cheap on the basis they helped paint it. It was big enough to house their art-school friends who would all come and live there at different times.

Mum painted and looked after us, and Dad taught at the Canterbury College of Art. This was a considerable distance, especially as he didn't drive, so he would be away for most of the week. Dad recruited some of his students to form a band and they would come back to the vicarage to practise on the weekends. Eventually they began to play a few gigs around the pub circuit in London and their sheer improbability became their strength as they slowly started to attract larger audiences. Dad couldn't sing in what was considered a conventional way but compensated for it by writing brilliantly witty lyrics, and he assumed the persona of a sort of homeless magician. The band was made up of an assortment of other unlikely characters that never looked like they were meant to be on a stage. Malcolm McLaren, the future manager of the Sex Pistols, would watch eagerly, bringing people like John Lydon to admire Dad's stagecraft as the Kilburns unconsciously contributed to the first stages of what would become punk music. Eventually Dad's focus shifted from teaching to the idea that this could be his job.

He met the much younger Denise at the Lord Nelson pub in Holloway Road while playing a gig and his desire to be away from home grew. Mum was non-confrontational and she let him be who he thought he had to be, and on the odd occasion when he returned she would still iron his shirts for the following night's gig. The last time he came back to the vicarage was the day before the Kilburns went off to support the Who on the UK leg of their tour. In August 1974, Dad moved into a tiny flat in one of the Oval Mansions council blocks overlooking the cricket ground in Vauxhall.

Mum, Jemima and I were left destitute without any source of income except the social security benefits we received due to having an absent father. Dad would only visit occasionally so as not to alert the authorities that he was still in contact. We moved from the beautiful vicarage to an isolated cottage in a neighbouring village called Puttenham. Bits of disused agricultural machinery were strewn around the muddy field that surrounded the desolate house. We survived off the occasional trip to a cash-and-carry where Mum bought catering packs of cheap food. Jemima's school was a two-mile walk and we didn't have a car. Mum was attacked by a local farmer, possibly in the house we were living in. I'm not sure to what extent as it was never discussed with us but I get the feeling it must have been a very desperate time for Mum at this point. After eighteen months, and with financial support from Aunt Moll, we moved to Mount Pleasant in Aylesbury into our first proper home.

Dad had committed himself to being a singer. He

ruthlessly practised his performance skills and the band continually played. He went through many different musicians, managers and stage person-alities until he eventually dismantled the Kilburns in favour of a new direction. In the four years of relentless touring he learned his craft and built a reputation as a fascinating frontman unlike anyone before him. Mum and Dad maintained a closeness and he would come to Aylesbury intermittently for periods of restorative family life and would work on his lyrics. He found a new writing partner called Chaz Jankel who was young and confident enough to shield himself from Dad's volatility. They collab-orated for a year before putting down the ten songs they co-wrote with three hired session musicians from a funk band called Loving Awareness. One half of Dad's new management, Peter Jenner, who had a history working with Pink Floyd and Marc Bolan, helped force a direction in the recording process. To limit expenditure and time he allowed only two overdubs per track, which concentrated the arrangements and gave the album a sparseness that made it sound unique and exciting.

I happened to be with Dad for the weekend when the album photoshoot took place and as a result ended up on the front cover. This was an accident as I had shyly walked into shot, as Dad explained later, but I have no memory of it at all. I do remember the attention I got from it afterwards, which I really enjoyed but didn't really understand.

New Boots and Panties!!, released in 1977, went on to be Dad's biggest selling album and stayed in the top ten for over a year. Loving Awareness were hired as a live band and were renamed the Blockheads, and they toured the album without stopping for two years. This slowly but surely changed everything for Dad, and also for us as a family. He started to make money and it trickled back towards us. Life changed shape in incremental stages. A car and holidays – the sort of things we had never even dreamed of owning or experiencing – came into our lives.

Mum bought a second-hand beige Morris Minor minivan and put a mattress in the back so Jemima and I could sleep on long journeys. Dad, after all his displacement, decided to move into a suite in the Dorchester Hotel. Mum would drive the new Morris Minor up to the grand entrance just off Park Lane. The hotel porter would look uncomfortable as Jemima and I leapt out the back, unsuitably dressed and wild eyed. The first thing we would do was order a club sandwich and drink as much Coca-Cola as possible. Dad was embarrassed about having money and he tried to get rid of it as quickly as he made it, so everything in those days seemed staggeringly over the top.

5

ROLVENDEN

Rolvenden, Kent, 1978

Toad Hall, Rolvenden, was a modern red-brick mansion in the heart of Kent with an Olympic-size swimming pool and various outbuildings. In preparation for the follow-up to *New Boots and Panties!!* Dad decided to house the entire band together and create a work residency. Various rooms were adapted into studios to allow each of the band members to work on songs, which gave them a chance to be part of the larger picture. They were

handed a lyric and a brief, and Dad would period-
ically check on their progress in a similar way he
would have taught at art school.

At the same time I was suffering at my school
in Aylesbury. I would go missing halfway through
a lesson. I have the vaguest memory of hiding on
top of a toilet cubicle while everyone was desperately looking for me. Once or twice I just walked
home without telling the teacher. Mum became
increasingly worried and appealed to Dad for some
help and suggested he needed to be more involved
in my life. He, in his unconsidered and enthusiastic way, proposed that I go and live with him in
Rolvenden and enlist in the local school. So at the
age of seven and with both parents in agreement I
was uprooted from my home and sent to stay with
Dad, his band, their wives and girlfriends, and Dad's
new girlfriend, Helga, who had two boys.

At first this all seemed like a great idea. There
was a continual throng of partially dressed adults
in and out of the pool, all revelling in the novelty
of their new surroundings. For the first month there
were some other children there because it was
the summer holidays. They included the energetic
Alfie Rowe, who was a little younger than me and

the son of Fred 'Spider' Rowe, Dad's minder at the time. Alfie would tear around the grounds without a flicker of concern for his or anyone else's safety until he was forcibly subdued by an adult. Then he would bite someone or something, once taking a mouth-sized chunk out of the back of the leather seat in the Volvo Fred was driving.

Fred himself was mostly calm but always carried the faint presence of violence within him. His ergonomic body shape was designed for fighting. He was short, compact and bald, and looked like a Victorian boxer. He had an alertness about him and was wary of his surroundings, probably from time spent in prison or around other hostile career criminals. He was perfectly suited to supervising Dad's mercurial nature and mostly would minimise the drama, but he could also really fuck people up if necessary.

They had met as neighbours when Fred lived below Dad in the Oval Mansions in Vauxhall and caught his attention when he replaced his front windows with bulletproof security glass. Dad, intrigued by his shadowy neighbour, began to talk to him and they soon became friends. He discovered that Fred had just finished a ten-year stretch in Parkhurst prison for a failed armed robbery. Fred Rowe was usually the member of Johnny Pyatt's safe-cracking gang sent up a drainpipe to disarm alarms, hence the nickname Spider, but on that occasion he was the getaway driver. His two armed colleagues managed to get the money into the back of Fred's car before they were both arrested. Fred drove all the way to Glasgow and hid £30,000 in two biscuit tins at his Aunty Ethel's house – this was a considerable amount of cash back then. He was arrested on his return to London, tried and sentenced.

His two colleagues sent a clear message to Fred that they expected their money on release and, in the meantime, as long as it was safe, so was he. Two years into their sentence, Aunty Ethel passed away. In a desperate panic Fred managed to get hold of his law-abiding brother Dell and explain his dilemma that if anyone found the money he would get killed in prison. His brother accepted that he had to retrieve the money and drove to Glasgow that night just in time to find Aunty Ethel's two sisters clearing out her house, with the two biscuit tins just about to be opened. He scooped up the two tins, returned home and buried them in his garden, to be forgotten about until 1971, the year Britain was turning decimal. The money had to be laundered into small denominations via hundreds of different grocery shops all over England in order to convert it to the new currency. Dell managed to change the majority of the original haul and reburied it back in his garden. A few years later, Fred and his two colleagues were released and Fred managed to persuade the other two that it was honourable to give Dell a percentage of the money, considering his work involved in preserving it.

After his stretch, Fred was at a crossroads. Dad admired anyone able-bodied and potentially violent. He slightly fantasised about their potential role in his world and persuaded Fred to go straight and work for him. On the landmark occasion when Fred bought a new fridge-freezer for the first time, using money he'd earned working for Dad, he apparently had a small cry as this was beyond his expectations.

Chaz Jankel brought Monti, his Great Dane, to Toad Hall and I loved him, but sometimes Monti would become overexcited and was difficult to control. On one occasion after Monti and I were playing he stood up on his hind legs and used his front paws to push me down on the floor and became very aroused. Dad shouted at Fred to do something so he punched Monti directly on his nose. Monti stiffened, made a tiny whimpering sound and fell sideways unconscious. Fred didn't always act gracefully but the circumstances weren't always easy for him to calculate appropriately. He tried his best and never without considering all the options.

Once the other children had gone and the adult festivities faded, the house became emptier and I was left without much to do. Dad, Chaz, Micky and the other Blockheads – Norman Watt-Roy, Charlie Charles and John Turnbull – all set to work writing and playing. There was a strong work ethic from Dad and Chaz, who were competing with their own previous achievements after the success of *New Boots*. Chaz wrote the arrangement to 'Hit Me with Your Rhythm Stick' in those sessions, and both he and Dad recognised its potential to be their next single.

The only thing I remember from the studio was Charlie, the Blockheads' drummer, playing with an echo machine while I was in another room. He put himself on the large speakers and repeatedly called out my name. The delayed effect made it spiral off into an unimaginable soundscape. I was so delighted by it I made him do it over and over again until everyone was exhausted and told him to stop.

I started Rolvenden Primary School with Helga's two sons, which is when it became apparent how homesick I was. The teachers looked at us in despair as though we were from a cult, which we sort of were. I had no real idea who Helga was at the time or why she had been given the authority to look after me. She had a strong German accent and a no-nonsense austerity about her. I didn't like her from the very moment I met her, not because I was territorial over Dad – he'd had plenty of girlfriends, especially since he'd become more famous. But maybe she had been put in an awkward position of responsibility in having to look after me when she was hoping for more frolics of a rock 'n' roll nature, and in turn was a little cold.

In the excitement of writing 'Hit Me with Your Rhythm Stick' Dad and the band vacated Toad Hall to record the song in London. I was left alone with Helga and her two sons. Helga, without anyone else around, became everything I feared. On the first night without Dad around she tried to force-feed me lentils. Never in all my pampered years had I tasted something so foul. We hadn't been affected by any progressive cooking at Mum's. We ate simply and probably unhealthily, but this was a leap too far. When Helga left the room I began slowly to distribute the lentils in small amounts to the two cats underneath the dinner table. Helga's two sons told her what I was doing and she shouted at me in German and sent me up to my room. I tried to switch on the lamp in the darkness and managed to put my finger on an un-bulbed socket, which electrocuted me. I erupted uncontrollably and didn't stop crying until the next day.

Helga's hatred grew as she hadn't catered for the levels of distress I was capable of inflicting. The following weeks were painful for both of us until eventually Mum came and got me. I'm not sure if Dad ever returned to Toad Hall or what happened to Helga but good fucking riddance – not to her, as it probably wasn't her fault, but to that situation. Why I was left in the care of a stranger for so long is still a mystery.

6

CONSEQUENCES OF FAME

Aylesbury and Abroad, 1979

If things hadn't changed enough already, the success of 'Hit Me' meant that our family was never the same. Six months after the stay at Toad Hall, on 27 January 1979, it went to number one, eventually selling way over a million copies. Not that I as a seven-year-old had any great acknowledgement of this but everyone appeared happier around us. It meant that Jemima and I would see Dad less and less and only at opportune moments, usually backstage before a gig. Even then we were palmed off with a management lackey or a minder. If we were lucky, it was Kosmo Vinyl that would look after us. He was Dad's unofficial press officer and just nineteen years old, and to me he was just like the Fonz. He had a cheekiness about him that made him, in comparison to some of the facile men in Dad's entourage, more joyful to be around. I remember him taking me to see *Star Wars* at the Leicester Square Odeon and telling me in great detail that it was the last place that Spider had robbed before going to prison, which I was so impressed by.

On my eighth birthday I was given a Scalextric racing set, at the time an unimaginably expensive present, and thrown a party in Mount Pleasant. The whole street attended – Colin, James, Rafael, even Fontaine Carter. We as a family suddenly were the centre of attention in our relatively poor and uneventful corner of Aylesbury. For Dad to have a number-one record and to be on *Top of the Pops* every week was ultimate fame. But we still lived on the same street and still had the same friends, and Jemima and I were relatively oblivious to the consequences of being wealthier. We did suddenly have more than those around us who didn't have much but Mum was determined to make us aware of that and made sure we shared everything – against our wishes. Yet sometimes people threw stones at our car just because they thought we were different now.

Dad organised an event for all the local children before playing at the Friars, Aylesbury's local venue. It was in recognition of the community in which Mum, Jemima and I had lived for the last few years and a celebration of the band's success. A Punch and Judy show was the main attraction. I had suddenly become a bit more obnoxious and arrogantly hurled abuse at the puppeteer mid show without any fear of being told off. The puppeteer's head appeared from below the small wooden stage. He removed his balaclava and appealed for me and my friends to stop swearing at him. Spider arrived just in time to escort us out before telling the poor puppeteer, 'Just carry on, mate, and stop worrying,' in a slightly threatening tone.

That night the Blockheads played a blazing set at the peak of their career. Even as a child I was mesmerised by their expertise in overwhelming an audience. Dad would lurk between the sharp light and darkness of a stage and then suddenly lean into focus as a song's tension developed. The Blockheads were always ready to let go but never before the moment of impact, and between Dad and the band there was a perfectly timed assault. The crowd were left in a state of euphoria, unable to suppress their excitement afterwards, and that's when things could get tricky. At the time anything punk related seemed to attract a fascistic following, especially in the more rural areas. This made no sense as the Blockheads were made up of an ethnic mix and their music had more to do with jazz and funk. In my memory, that night a group of skinheads overwhelmed the backstage security guards and started charging up and down the corridors. Pip, a kindly roadie, grabbed Jemima and me, shoved us into an empty room and wedged a table against the door. He sat with his back to the table and told us funny stories to keep us distracted. Spider and a few of his men restored order.

Not that long after, Jemima, our two family friends Emily and Joel and I went on a UK tour in an impromptu arrangement Dad made with Mum and their parents. This may have overlapped with school time but no one seemed to care that much in those days. Dad craved our company more than ever as he was rarely at home and was burned out from nonstop travelling. But as expected he took little responsibility in overseeing our welfare during this time, and we were shoved around between an assortment of different managers, minders, girl-friends and roadies, some more begrudging than others. We were with each other, though, so my memory of the tour is still fantastic.

When we arrived at the Turnberry hotel near Aberdeen, we were left under the protection of Little Chris, who had a kind of junior minder's role. He was a cocky miscreant from Brixton who had won a few boxing competitions but had no under-standing of the formalities of caring for children. He took us down to the shore supposedly to collect shells. When Jemima found a large jellyfish caught on the rocks he produced a serrated combat knife and sliced it into four quarters. Joel and I thought this was hilarious but Jemima was horrified and ran back to the hotel to find Dad. I'm not sure if Dad did anything; he most likely thought it was necessary for us to understand people like Little Chris. In Little Chris's defence he was only sixteen years old and had no idea what he was doing. He has ever since been a charming person to know.

We sometimes slept in a formation around Dad's hotel room in any shape possible. I would always opt for the foot of the bed and sleep widthways. Jemima and Emily would try to top-to-toe on the sofa and Joel would make a mattress out of the spare pillows and sleep on the floor. When my clothes became too smelly to continue wearing I was bought a new football kit in whatever city/town we were in.

After a couple of weeks on the road we dropped Emily and Joel back with their parents and then flew to Zurich where one of Dad's girlfriends, Zenia, looked after us. She discouraged our Coca-Cola drinking and made us eat something healthy. She was bossier than some of the others but seemed more concerned about our welfare.

Jemima and I were put to bed in an adjoining suite next to Dad's room when he went off to play the gig. I have a hazy recollection of being woken up by a silhouetted figure sitting at the end of our bed. Dad had his head in his hands and was crying. We switched on the lights and he shuffled up between us and cuddled us while he carried on crying. In his suite next to us was the sound of people drinking as the smoke floated underneath the door. He began to tell us jokes to lighten the atmosphere. 'Who wants a skid-mark sandwich? . . . Who wants big numpties?' We laughed till our sides split and fell back to sleep on either side of him. Success means an endless toil that results in a crash, and he was crashing.

Then we went to Rome for a day. We spent the entire time at a TV studio while the Blockheads rehearsed a song that would later be filmed live in front of an audience. We scurried around making a nuisance of ourselves, annoying the Italian techs. Eventually we were ushered into a room with a bank of television screens and told to be quiet. The show started with a performance from an Italian rock band who were dressed in skin-tight, sparkly chrome outfits with high-heel boots and bleach-blond Mohicans. The lead singer walked on carrying a large tube covered in the same chrome material and pointed it at the audience like it was a gun. He pressed down on a lever and it released a series of sparks. A second later the sparks turned into a long flame that jetted out further than he was expecting and hit the nearest audience member directly in the face. I stared in horror as the image of her burned face appeared on each television screen in front of us. Pip the roadie grabbed both of us from behind, covered our eyes and gently pushed us out of the room. The show was cancelled. We left Rome the next morning without seeing any of it.

At the end of 1979 we went to Barbados for a month. It was the first time Jemima and I had been on a real holiday. Mum, Jemima and I went out early to stay in a beautiful villa on the west coast right next to the Sandy Lane Hotel. We had our own cook and a guard who had a large rod of bamboo with a big, jagged fish hook on the end. Dad, the band and their families were to follow a couple of weeks later, I believe all at Dad's expense.

After a week we were told that Hurricane David was heading in our direction and that preparations were being made to evacuate the coastal areas. Fortunately, Mum had an old friend that had lived on the island for the last ten years so we moved to her centrally located house. Alison ran an art school for the locals on the less touristy side of Barbados. A day before the storm was expected, she took Jemima and me to visit some of her students' families to try to persuade them to take refuge in the sturdier school building as they were living in fragile shacks. She wanted us to see the realities of the divided island – the Bajans hissed at us as we drove past and we were generally unwelcome. Several labourers spent hours boarding up Alison's house until we were totally concealed inside. Jemima and I huddled up to Mum and fell asleep while she waited all night, anxiously awake. The storm took a sharp turn towards Dominica and flattened it, killing lots of people, and Barbados was left relatively unharmed.

Dad and the band turned up a few days later, oblivious to what we had just been through. They mostly occupied one enormous villa, except for Dad who stayed in the regal Sandy Lane Hotel. While most of the adults partied I played with a tiny lamb called Larry who ran freely around the backyard of the villa until Spider picked him up one afternoon and said, 'That's your lunch, son. Don't get too attached.' He went behind the shed and slaughtered him. I didn't stop crying for the rest of the holiday.

When we got back to Aylesbury, the Sadiq family had loaded up a rusting white Bedford van and were about to drive to Pakistan to see their family. Jemima had successfully applied to the Arts Educational School to study ballet and Dad had agreed to pay for it. Mum had found a new house close to the school in Tring, a slightly posher town in the neighbouring county of Hertfordshire. So that was the end of Aylesbury and the last time I would see Colin and James for a year.

7

GRAFFITI

━━━━━━

Chiswick, London, early 1980s

Graffiti was an escape from the things I hated about Chiswick School as I managed to broaden my social group and find more like-minded friends. Toby was in the year above. He was always immaculately dressed with perfectly combed hair and had the appearance of a nerd but for the colourful letters beautifully drawn on the back of his rucksack indicating his other interests. We quickly discovered that we were both into graffiti and formed a partnership; he wrote 'Dare' and I became 'Agro', which accurately described our personalities.

Toby's family were hard-working people who had made the best of their situation. Their house was full of shiny ornaments and was always surgically clean, unlike either of my parents' houses. Jenny, his mother, would make us tiny, triangular-shaped sandwiches with a thin layer of salmon paste in them like you were at a funeral.

The two most important factors to graffiti were coverage or bombing, which meant the amount you could tag, and the more creative side: attempting to find a fresh, untouched surface, as exposed as possible, on which to put a designed piece of art-work. This second factor obviously had many more considerations to it and was potentially dangerous. The main focus for most writers was to emulate the New York-style approach on its subway system, as having a tag or a whole artwork on a train carriage that travelled through different boroughs gave the most exposure possible. Access to the train depots or, as they were known colloquially, the yards was still complicated and only for the reckless. The third rail of most electric trains is the source of its power and will kill you instantly. You could theoretically, if wearing the correct footwear, jump on the third rail with both feet making contact at the same time but any tiny misjudgement would be fatal. A few kids did do that and there were some that died. I never once considered it. A lot of this side of graffiti was more about adrenalin than trying to piece a train. So to express ourselves creatively we went to unofficially designated areas, usually old building developments like the Sundance in Hammersmith or the Hall of Fame in Ladbroke Grove, where graffiti was more tolerated.

Our ambition was to collect as much spray paint as possible over a period of time and then find a clean wall to piece on. Spray paint came in many different formats but the easiest to steal was car paint, mostly used for retouching scratches. This was a cheap, metallic-based aerosol that was thin and hard to use, and looked shit. Buntlack, an acrylic-based art spray, had a much thicker coverage and a slower pressured output so was easier to control, but that was very expensive and hard to find. Toby and I would ransack a local art shop in Chiswick, using various ploys to distract the shop owner. We could walk out with two or three cans shoved down each sleeve. Toby was always much braver than I was and looked more presentable so got away with it, whereas I just had a troubled face.

Toby and I grew in notoriety and eventually teamed up with Declan, who wrote 'Vision'. We became known as Graphically Insane and started to become recognised around west London, even being mentioned on Tim Westwood's pirate radio station LWR, at the time the height of recognition.

Declan was from a hard Irish family that lived on the Hammersmith end of the Fulham Palace Road. His dad was a builder and he knew that sooner or later he would be as well. But he was a natural artist and a fearless tagger. He had an effervescent character that remained positive in contrast to his stark home life. He always managed to brighten up the dour Toby or the worrisome me and was a joy to be around.

Sundance was a disused car park in-between King Street in the centre of Hammersmith and the District and Piccadilly tube line. It was owned by the London Transport Authority but had been left to ruin for years. It had several large arches underneath the elevated track that would have stored rail equipment years ago but were now abandoned to homeless people. It was a perfect place to paint as it could be seen from the tube trains but was neglected enough for the graffiti police to be unconcerned by it. Every writer made a pilgrimage to Sundance but for us it was our local haunt and we spent as much time as possible among the decay.

One day we arrived and there was a bus parked under one of the arches. A bony, topless man with dirty long hair and soiled jeans was washing his clothes in a basin of brown water. He looked up at us with haunted eyes and an unkindly face. His small dog was tied to the end of the bus with a ragged piece of rope. The dog growled at us when we all leapt over the wall. Declan, who was always vocal, shouted a few insults and then we carried on, put up some tags and inspected the walls. Then Toby screamed for us to run. I was the furthest away from the man but also, unfortunately, the exit. The man had let the tiny dog off its rope lead and it sprinted around the circumference of the derelict square, cornering me on one side of it. The dog jumped up at my left thigh, dug his teeth into my flesh and then locked his mouth. Declan ran behind it and kicked it as hard as he could, and the dog squealed as it released its jaws and ran back towards his master, who was still staring at us with his horrible eyes. We retreated back over the wall and I went to Charing Cross Hospital to get a tetanus injection.

The following week we reconvened and, in light of what had happened, brought more people. As we entered the square the man was nowhere to be seen but next to his bus was a large pan of boiling water over a makeshift fire. We calmly spread ourselves around the square but remained alert. Declan, upset by what had happened the previous week, marched towards the stove and decided to kick over the pan of boiling water. From the back of the bus the man appeared with his snarling dog on a rope. He let go of the dog and ran towards Declan with his hair flailing in the air. Declan managed to swerve past him and run back towards the wall and leap over it in one go. Panic took over, with everyone sprinting in different directions. I started to climb a pile of rubble to see if I could make it to the fence that divided Sundance from the main road. Everyone else had made it back over the wall and was shouting at me to look behind. I managed to get to the top of the pile and grab hold of the fence but then my knee gave way. A shocking pain ran through my whole body and I smashed down on bits of broken glass and metal. I turned my body round just as the man reached me. He stood above me, bare-chested like he was Charles Manson, and stared into my eyes as he gasped for breath.

I screamed loudly at him, 'Pleeeease, you've got to help me, pleeeease don't hurt me,' hoping to find any trace of humanity in him. I was convinced he was going to pick up a brick and smash it down on to my skull. Everyone was shouting at him from behind but too scared to approach.

His eyes dropped and he suddenly looked forlorn and uncertain of what he was doing. Declan was the first one to reach me and started to drag me off the bricks. The man walked slowly back towards his bus where the dog was still snarling. My friends carried me down the high street back towards Charing Cross Hospital, where I'd been the week before at exactly the same time. I was kept there for a few days while small metal pins were put in my kneecap.

Dad loved Declan and thought graffiti was a form of rebel art that was to be encouraged. He had years ago commissioned Luke and me to paint 'Ladbroke Groove', an old song title, in his spare room. Declan would come over to the Hammersmith flat and smoke pot with me and sometimes Dad. He was equally impressed and frightened by Dad, like most of my friends, but Dad never picked on Declan, which was a rare compliment. We were probably unlike any folk Declan had met before and he had a few experiences that he'd never forget, like the time we met Clover.

One Saturday afternoon in the midst of summer, Dad, Declan and I were sitting on the balcony smoking a big spliff, quietly admiring the view. In the distance was an unusual chugging sound coming from up the river towards Putney. The shape of the vessel was unique and appeared to have the front bonnet of a jeep. The sound grew louder as it approached Hammersmith Bridge, at which point it turned towards the flat. A large fat man stood up from what looked like a normal steering wheel and waved frantically at us.

'Ian, it's me. It's Clover, it's Clover.'

The contraption then emerged from the water and drove up the bank directly outside the balcony.

'Ian, it's me, it's Clover. I've bought an amphibious duck . . . '

Dad looked stunned and whispered to Declan

and me, who both couldn't quite believe what we were seeing, 'Fuck, it's Clover. He's a lunatic ... Hello, Clover, what the fuck is that?'

It had three sets of wheels and looked like a bastardised Land Rover. It had faded traces of camouflage all over it.

'It's my duck, Ian. I've come to get you. We're going to Richmond,' Clover said in the deepest cockney accent.

It was obvious that Dad wasn't going to get on Clover's duck. 'You must be fucking joking, mate. I'm not getting in that thing but ... ' He paused for a moment and then said, 'My son will and his mate Declan will, won't you boys?'

Clover turned out to be a low-level gangster who had bought a floating military vehicle to avoid the police. While being chased, he would slip into the Thames, re-emerging on the other side, and then disappear. Or so he said.

There were two other people on the boat. One was a very large and boisterous lady who proclaimed she was an actress. The other was an impossibly thin man with a giant Adam's apple who said nothing at all the entire trip except for when he sang.

'Oh my, you're simply wonderful young men,' said the actress over and over again.

Clover gave us a glass of champagne each and we set off at an impossibly slow pace, stopping at almost all the pubs that were accessible en route. We drank pint after pint after pint as Clover and the actress told us fantastically inappropriate stories about their lives. Crowds gathered around us each time we climbed the bank and sometimes Clover would generously take people on trips across the river and back.

On our return it was pitch black except for the tiny red lights either side of the bridges indicating which lane of the river you should be in. Both Declan and I were now drunk and steering the duck while the three other very unlikely friends sang in the back, the actress being the loudest. Every now and then Clover would lean into me and say, 'Fucking Dunkirk, this cunt, fucking . . . fucking your dad, he's the fucking one . . . Dunkirk, eh?'

Dad never explained how he knew Clover or what his real occupation was, but in the few hours Declan and I spent with him he was thoroughly charming.

Holland Park School, London

Toby introduced me to some of his other friends who went to Holland Park School. It was an entirely different world from Chiswick and suddenly I found people that were actually similar to the way I was.

Holland Park was a state school and its unique location, in between Kensington and Ladbroke Grove, meant its socioeconomic catchment area was more diverse than other parts of London. The school tried to reflect this in the way it functioned. It had by the late 1970s abandoned any competitive streaming in favour of what it called 'egalitarianism' in order not to demoralise the low achievers. It scrapped the uniform and any religious affiliations. The school was initially a flagship of modern thinking but by the mid-eighties had started to stagnate. It was full of second-generation hippy kids whose parents had made Notting Hill their playground in the sixties. It was here that the dream maybe came to an end as the children tried to untangle some of their parents' less plausible lifestyle choices. But it wasn't just hippy kids as Ladbroke Grove and its surrounding areas had Jamaican, Moroccan and Portuguese communities whose kids also attended.

Then there were the rich kids from Kensington or Chelsea whose mums and dads were film directors or fashion designers with lefty leanings. By the time I discovered it, it was like a Shangri-La in its last throes.

The grisly realities of Chiswick weren't to be seen in Holland Park, which, even though it was chaotic and sometimes rough, had a hope about it. It was racially mixed and it was accepting of sexuality in all forms. Built on the edge of a Victorian park that served as its playground, the peacocks roamed freely and the teachers smoked pot with the pupils.

Toby's friend Saul was kind and gentle. His parents were university lecturers who lived in a nice house on the borders of Hammersmith and Shepherd's Bush. He was enviously cool without trying. He wore a Che Guevara beret and was handsome: he looked like a poster boy for a revolution. At the time, he was the only one of us to have a girlfriend, Lisa, who lived in Streatham with her Swedish mum. Her Jamaican dad had disappeared long before. Ben lived next door to Saul. He was exceptionally smart and went to a private school called Latimer but tried to disguise his accent with something he considered more street so he felt like he was one of us, but we were all pretending as well.

And then there was Zenaide, who became my best friend. He was the definition of Holland Park School. He was tall and athletic with a Swiss mum and possibly a Spanish dad. He'd never actually met his dad and had only pieced together fragments of information over the years from family friends. Michele, his mother, was a formidable force of courage who had persevered through some tough conditions to rear Zenaide in the best way she could. Originally from the small town of Delemont, she had fled the orderly culture of Switzerland to pursue a migratory lifestyle, ending up flitting between London and the Balearic island of Formentera, where possibly Zenaide was conceived on a beach. They lived on Rucklidge Avenue in the then tough streets of Harlesden. He was a very popular figure at Holland Park, being able to connect with all the different camps. His leopard-skin glasses, Brylcreemed quiff and vintage brogues created a trademark look, like a Beat Generation Clark Kent.

Zenaide and I had an instant bond when we first met. There was something in common that we both related to in our childhood experience. Even though he never had the financial cushion that I had, there was a shared uncertainty. We became and remained very close like brothers, and we can bicker like brothers too.

Zen was greatly admired around Ladbroke Grove, gaining respect from the scarier elements as I perceived them. There were different gangs and supposedly more dangerous characters but all of them had time for Zenaide. I was essentially playing catch-up on how to look and act cool but to Zenaide and a lot of the kids at Holland Park it was inherently natural and a part of their development. I was rootless and contorted from life in Aylesbury, Tring and Chiswick, my clothes were wrong, my vocabulary outdated. I wasn't born in the heart of an inner-city bohemian village like Ladbroke Grove.

8

LIVING WITH DAD

Hammersmith, 1986

The end of Chiswick School was confirmed the day the deputy head rang. Unofficially, Dad's was now my refuge in the daytime as he understood that it was better for me being there than unaccountably lost on the streets. But the rules were not to bother him too early as the one pleasure success had afforded him was the right to stay in bed as late as he wanted.

When the phone rang I answered it without considering that most people who knew Dad would know he would still be asleep.

'Hi Baxter, is that you?' I didn't say anything. 'Baxter?'
I panicked and said, 'I'll get my dad.'

I woke Dad up as cautiously as I could.

'What time is it?'

'Eleven-thirty,' I said.

He didn't say anything and picked up the receiver and was about to speak. He looked up at me and mouthed the words 'Who is this?' I shrugged my shoulders but I knew who it was.

'Hello . . . ' he said with the least amount of effort. 'Right, I see . . . Yes, I do understand . . . Shit,' he said, which seemed inappropriate. 'OK, OK, well that can't be helped,' he said with a new spirit but then remained quiet for almost a minute as though he was listening. Then, 'WHY DON'T YOU FUCK OFF, YOU SNOTTY LITTLE MAGGOT.' His final touch was to slam down the phone.

'Make me a coffee,' he said.

Without any discussion, I hurried off in a state of shock and deeply upset about the slaying of the deputy head.

Dad's routines were born of a series of events that were unique to his life. He was equally brutalised and smothered in affection as a child and had strong tendencies towards both kindness and cruelty as a result. So to be around him was complicated and to be his son even more so. I accepted that I was marginalised by his need to do what he wanted first and then be a father later. His energy to succeed was a route to protecting himself against what he had suffered to get there. He was the solution to my chaos but maybe the source of it too.

Dad caught polio at the age of seven in an open-air swimming pool in Southend-on-Sea in 1949, just a few years before a vaccine was available. For six weeks he was encased in plaster and wasn't expected to live. When he pulled through he was sent to Black Notley Hospital in Braintree, Essex, close to where both of his now separated parents Bill and Peggy lived. For the next eighteen months he stayed bedbound with only a mirror above his bed to view the ward. Peggy had wanted him to become a lawyer and with her two sisters, Elizabeth and Molly, had taught him to read by the age of three. Aunt Moll, who worked for the education board, had discovered a special school in East Sussex where they helped disabled children to find a trade. Chailey Heritage Craft School was considered progressive when it was first conceived at the beginning of the twentieth century with the intention of assisting young boys with rickets, tuberculosis or malnutrition to become carpenters or bookbinders. But when Dad joined in 1951 as a nine-year-old with a withered left side it was a relic of Dickensian reform. The building was an old workhouse and its doctrine was to push the boys to grow strong through determination no matter what the obstacles were. The motto above the door was 'Men Are Made Here'. Pitted against different levels of mental and physical disability Dad learned to control his environment. Through combat or through wit he triumphed over an often sadistic regime of forced self-sufficiency. Abuse from the more able-bodied pupils or corrupt orderlies was tolerated and Dad eventually became less victim and more perpetrator. He grew necessarily unsympathetic to his surroundings in order to survive. Something in him was taken away in those years and replaced with something ruthlessly competitive.

The transition from living with Mum and attending Chiswick School to being at Dad's was totally seamless. I was far past the point of the everyday obedience required to survive within the loop of a normal school life. I had no respect for what I was told by most people and was never likely to achieve anything but upset if I had carried on. Dad's was the perfect environment to soak up all my energy and at the same time give me a ballast to hold on to. Even though unconventional in almost all of his habits, he demanded a lot from you and was always the boss. I did whatever Dad told me to without any hesitation as he had perfected the art of total control over everyone. But the clocks had turned upside down and I could live by the night in a new world, unflustered by the petty inconveniences that frustrated everyday folk. There was no school, there were no rules about drinking, there was no dinner, there was no morning hustle to get anywhere. The days unfolded at a different pace and the attention was now more on the evening, when anything could happen.

Hammersmith became a hub where my friends and I could be freer, but at the same time we became a part of Dad's entourage as the one thing he loved was attention. He was a pot-soaked Fagin character to us and our pact with him was to listen.

We would gather round, hanging on every word. He teased us with a brown envelope brimming with £50 notes, as we knew the one chosen to go to the off-licence would be rewarded with keeping the change. Booze, money and drugs feel so good when you are fourteen. When we were sufficiently stoned he would blow our minds with psychedelic jazz records by the likes of Roland Kirk.

Dad would conduct everything from his favourite seat in the music room, framed theatrically under a triangular prism of light created by an old Anglepoise lamp. The cannabis smoke would generate an atmospheric fog around his demonic smile and we were all mesmerised. A beautiful madness grew in the room and we carried on for hours until the banging at the front door became louder than us.

When it got really serious PC Honey would arrive. He was the local noise control officer. 'Ian, Baxter, is that you? I'm coming up,' he would say on the entry phone. He would walk through the front door, announce his arrival loudly and then sensitively pass the music room and go into the kitchen.

'Ian, I'm not coming into your room as I know what you're doing in there. I'm making a cup of tea.'

Then Dad would sheepishly greet him.

'Ian, come on, we've talked about this, haven't we?'

'Yeah, man,' Dad would say and smile lovingly at PC Honey.

After six months of officially not going to Chiswick School I was getting pretty bored. Each day was a struggle waiting for my friends to finish their lessons. I would hang out at the pool hall in the basement of Kensington Market, a dingy arcade where the kids from Holland Park would congregate. I would drink all day and then smoke a few spliffs with my friends until they were expected home at a reasonable hour. My endless freedom was starting to feel like a burden. Even when I was truanting at least I had a schedule of trying to avoid parents and teachers and stealing food.

Dad at the time was acting in a play called *Road*, written by Jim Cartwright, which explored the lives of the unemployed in a deprived town in Lancashire in the early 1980s under Thatcherism. He played Scullery, who narrated the story, and Jane Horrocks and Iain Glen were among the cast. After a successful run at the Royal Court Theatre they took the play to Copenhagen. Dad decided that it would be a good opportunity for me to go and help as I had fuck all to do.

Jane and Dad started dating and he remained relatively well behaved throughout the trip. I fetched his coffee, rolled spliffs and helped him on and off the stage. On stairs, Dad would be obsessed about the positioning of the banister and where it was in relation to which direction he was going. If the banister was on the left of the stairs going up it meant he'd use a walking stick to balance himself as his left side was affected by the polio. Or I'd help with his right strong hand on my left shoulder and the opposite going down. And when he did fall over, which happened quite often either due to something unforeseen or encouraged by drinking, I knew how to pick him up. I would place both hands under his arms from behind and walk forward while he stiffened both legs. I was effectively doing what a minder would have done over the years but I was cheaper and it wasn't necessary to have someone aggressive around in the softer world of theatre. It was inspirational to watch the show every night and see how the audience reacted. There was something very unique in the way the actors and crew behaved with each other after each perform-ance. It always felt celebratory and not like the sometimes unsympathetic backstage setting of a gig.

9

THE SULPHATE
STRANGLER AND BART

Hammersmith, 1986

The Sulphate Strangler arrived one afternoon at the Hammersmith flat. He was on his way to Portobello Market to collect some jewellery he was having custom made and wanted to see if I would go with him. He was dripping in different gold and silver pendants, necklaces, demonic earrings and turquoise arm bracelets. He had snakeskin cowboy boots over tight jeans with a gigantic silver skull centred on his belt buckle. His large belly was bulging through a floral shirt with the sleeves cut off, exposing his trunk-like arms.

Dad had a tactical interest in everyone's welfare. I suspect he had suggested I needed inspiring and thought Strangler also needed something to do so had contrived the day out.

Strangler, despite being threatening in size, was round-faced and bonny, and his demeanour was immediately infectious. He spoke without pausing and everything was funny. Dad struggled to keep up with his banter.

Before we left, Strangler grabbed Dad's hand and started to sing the 1950s song 'Shrimp Boats', and then they both moved in tiny synchronised steps and started to sing together. It may have been one of the funniest things I've ever seen.

The market was in full bloom in the mid-afternoon and everyone seemed to know Strangler. We arrived at a tiny jewellery shop under the Westway. A hollow-faced man with an ill-fitting leather jacket was hunched over, crafting the final details into a large chain. He looked at Strangler, grinned and said, 'Finally,' in an Eastern European accent. He placed his special engraving tool back on the desk, rose very slowly and said, 'This is really beautiful and I am so glad you have arrived today.'

He bent down and slid open a wide drawer full of detailed pieces and selected a necklace with a tiny silver tube at the end. Strangler picked it up and held it towards the light. He read out the minuscule inscription that curled round it: 'If you steal a little they'll put you in jail but if you steal a lot they'll make you a king.'

The Sulphate Strangler, originally named Pete Rush, was born to Jack and Marge in Bournemouth in 1951. As a child he suffered acute asthma and spent long periods of time in hospital. He attributed his tallness to the treatment they gave him and subsequently felt like an outsider. He never went back to school full time and ended up doing a few stretches in a young offenders' institute for burglary. By the age of fourteen he was hitchhiking up to London to watch his favourite bands. He would pester the road crews for work, eventually catching the attention of Led Zeppelin's lighting roadies who let him help set up the rigging and shut down the shows every night.

He stayed with the Zeppelin for several years,

learning everything there is about the road, drugs and the occult. The band's interests were shrouded in a dark mysticism that haunted Strangler for the rest of his life. He claimed he would deliver narcotics in the boot of his car to Jimmy Page's Scottish manor house. He was convinced that his eventual demise would be from the curse that was placed on everyone in the Zeppelin's employment at that time. He would repeatedly describe the incident in which a great friend was mown down on a zebra crossing for no reason by a car that was never traced. But they were doing a lot of LSD at the time, so much in fact that another of Strangler's repeated stories was about driving into the back of a bus on Oxford Street because he thought it was made out of rubber.

He went on to work with Thin Lizzy, Motörhead, Bob Marley, Siouxsie and the Banshees and many more before he became one of Dad's most committed people, depending on his state of mind.

He was christened the Sulphate Strangler by the infamous publicist B. P. Fallon while they were both working for Roy Harper. B. P. explained how Strangler's name evolved:

We find ourself in Norway with Roy playing to an antagonised crowd. The punters are not digging Roy's loud electric guitar meanderings so my request is 'More volume!' To ensure I'm understood, I shout out about the desired volume: 'Threshold of pain, please!' None of this is going down particularly well and a hulking Norwegian is threatening to give Roy a good kicking.

Pete springs into action, raising the annoying punter up by the neck until his face turns purple and his dangling feet are doing less twitching. 'Pete! Stop!' you yell to no effect. 'Pete, you're killing him!' No effect. 'All the punters can see you!' No effect. 'Pete, do it later!' This seems to Pete to be a sensible idea and he drops the semi-conscious punter to the ground and then precedes to forget all about the unfortunate creature.

Pete was not unknown to have a toot or three of sulphate – speed – to keep things lively. And thus after the shang-a-lang in Norway I titled him The Sulphate Strangler.

Strangler appeared more frequently over the next few months, helping Dad on different errands. He removed the for-sale signs outside Granny's flat in Hampstead and dumped them inside the premises of the estate agent responsible for erecting them. He chaperoned Dad while he appeared in *Hearts of Fire*, a film featuring Bob Dylan. They hung out in a trailer for a few days with Bob and Reg Presley from the Troggs. Bob immediately took a liking to Strangler and cast him in the film, which was by all accounts terrible.

Strangler would accompany Dad on his daily walk, usually through Richmond Park. He would turn up wearing silk skating shorts that revealed too much thigh and a pair of Second World War binoculars. Dad would walk at a meditative pace and it would take them a few hours to complete three or four miles. First stop was usually the Isabella Plantation to admire the evergreen azaleas and then through to the central woodland and possibly a rest at the ponds. Dad would smoke a big joint and discuss the mating habits of the great crested grebe while Strangler pretended to listen. At which point they headed back in the direction of Pembroke Lodge where they would have tea and scones with the old ladies at the café. Sometimes I was persuaded to accompany them for the benefit of having someone else to impress, and was once used as a decoy against an aggressive stag territorially protecting its young. I was forced out of the safety of the bench we had found to hide behind and drew the deer's attention away from Dad and Strangler. As soon as it shifted its focus, Dad and Strangler retreated back towards the woodland. I sprinted through the clearing to the nearest tree two hundred metres away and waited for half an hour while they went to the café.

Eventually Dad bought Strangler a tiny white Nissan Micra but with his enormous arms breaching either side of the vehicle it was almost impossible to sit next to him. Strangler placed a kamikaze flag across the front panel as a warning to everyone that he was potentially unstable. The Nissan was so remarkably small that it pacified the appearance of the Strangler, squashing his bouffant across the ceiling and softening his broken features. This led to the common mistake of overconfidence made by other drivers who he perceived were trying to provoke him. If they cut him up or beeped unjustifiably, Strangler's many earrings would start to chime as his head rolled from side to side. The mood would drop and the car would jolt forward. The aim was to trap the offender at a set of traffic lights, which would allow the Strangler to emerge from the car. From the perspective of the drivers, Strangler, silhouetted in the wing mirror, would appear like an orange Minotaur and they would inevitably jump the lights.

Dad decided to offer Strangler a room in the Hammersmith flat, which meant I had to move out of it. I was transferred on to the decaying Victorian daybed or, as Dad referred to it to make it sound more glamorous, the chaise longue in the front room. In a forced bonding exercise – or maybe Dad just wanted us out of the way – Strangler was told to take my friends and me out nightclubbing. Six of us managed to fit into the tiny white Nissan with Lisa, being the smallest, in the boot. Strangler gave us a few cans of Tennent's Super, which was an exceptionally strong lager often drunk by homeless people, to share. The first club we went to was called Across the Tracks at Dingwalls in Camden. Everyone knew Strangler and we were ushered in without any issue. We were given a drink each by the bar staff amused by our age and told to stay close to one another on the dancefloor while Strangler attended to some business. We tentatively started to dance, each showing our potential. The beer had made us feel a little drunk and the music sounded incredible.

After a while, I could see Strangler towards the back of the nightclub, and his head was moving erratically from side to side. A small crowd of people had formed a circle around him and his mammoth arms were stretched out with his hands gripped around someone's neck. As I approached I could see the fear in the other man's eyes. We all gathered behind Strangler, forming an orderly line. Strangler ordered us to start heading towards the exit. 'It's out of order,' is all he said to his victim, over and over again. He let go of the man, who slumped to the floor. The club security stepped aside and we walked past them calmly. We all suspected Strangler was mad but now we knew it.

We dared not say anything as we got back into the Nissan. He slammed down the accelerator and sped across London. We arrived at the Slimelight club which was three floors of frightening goths in an old church. Their eyes seemed to glow and their bodies merged into the darkness like owls. This was more Strangler's comfort zone as the first club was maybe for our benefit. Strangler was still agitated, though, and it was clear this wasn't a place to bring six children. We were told to be quiet and sit at a table, and he gave us a flask of vodka to share. He went into the darker fringes of the club and wasn't seen again for an hour as the goths looked at us disapprovingly. He came back and sat on the table and used the silver tube attached to the necklace to sniff up some white powder from a tiny plastic vial. He looked around as though he felt it impolite not to offer us any and then decided against it.

On the way home Strangler, now more upbeat, stopped on the All Saints Road in Ladbroke Grove. He waited for all the drug dealers to gather round the car and then wound down the window and hollered, 'Grrrrrrooooooaaaarrrrgh.' He sped the car for a short distance and then stopped and waited for the dealers to start chasing us, and then repeated this several times. We genuinely screamed for our lives and didn't enjoy one second of it until we were safely out of danger and then thought it was hilarious.

After a few months of living with Strangler I started to grow accustomed to his vast range of habits. He often took amphetamines in the morning in the same way someone would drink coffee. If he took too much he would stabilise this with alcohol, which was impractical during the day, especially if he had errands to do for Dad. Sometimes he would have a Special Brew before noon, and then consume a whole Ventolin inhaler, or two if stressed, in the afternoon. Speed is an appetite suppressant so he wouldn't eat anything all day. His fluctuating weight was always a concern so he saw this as a benefit.

By early evening he'd have a few more lines and would start to get a bit jittery, at which point he'd have to drink stronger alcohol. He would swig from a bottle of Jack Daniel's that he concealed in his room.

To sleep he would take a handful of temazepam. They were green rubbery capsules known as jellies, that contained a liquid barbiturate. This would cancel out all the speed and shut down his system for a few hours. And so the cycle would continue.

Contrary to his violent persona, Strangler enjoyed being domestic and we would go shopping every Saturday morning. First stop, Safeway Supermarket, so we would drive the short distance to the Hammersmith mall car park. Gravy granules, potatoes, frozen peas, various meat pies and shampoo. He would growl at the other shoppers who gawped for too long. We would queue up and the checkout person would register each product while staring at him. He kept all his cash in a tightly rolled wad in a money bag concealed under his testicles. He would delve inside his pink boxer shorts to retrieve it and their mouth would drop in shock and disgust but they would politely accept the cash in order not to offend the giant. Next, we would go to Marks & Spencer and, in Strangler's eyes, encounter a better class of shopper, and as a result he behaved less conspicuously.

On occasion we would go to meet Graham, who was an amphetamine manufacturer with a big house opposite the bottom end of Hampstead Heath. Graham was quiet, unassuming and enormously polite. Nothing about him suggested he made or sold drugs. I guess that I was taken as a way of lessening suspicion if we were pulled over by the police. I was told strictly to never mention these visits to Dad or anyone else.

Strangler would drive under different aliases depending on which country or county he was in. His real name was Pete Rush, which he still used, but most of the time he was Christopher Ingrams or Brian Granger. I had to be very sure of remembering this.

An Aboriginal man called Bartholomew arrived at the flat one afternoon. He was small and athletic with a huge wave of black hair and colossal sideburns. Dad had met him several years before while touring in Australia. He leapt around enthusiastically explaining his heritage, encouraged by Dad who must have heard most of it before. It transpired that Bartholomew belonged to one of the last active tribes somewhere in Tasmania. He told us how to spear a crocodile from a canoe, and that you should lick a hallucinogenic frog's back. Dad tried to interest Strangler but he just withdrew back into my old room, now his drug cave.

After a certain point of drinking, Dad's behaviour became a lottery. It was best not to underestimate how crazy he could turn so, as usual, I faded into the front room without being noticed. The rotting chaise longue was one of only two bits of furniture that existed in the barren room. There were no curtains so the light was tormentingly bright from the crack of dawn. Sleep was an art form among all the disruptions posed by natural and human interruptions.

A thunderous banging woke me up a short while later. Someone was slamming their fist on the front door and ringing the bell. As I tentatively approached I could see the outline of the upstairs neighbour through the frosted glass. I opened the door and saw he had a hammer in his right hand. I shouted for Dad but he wasn't in the music room where I'd left him. An ominous sound permeated the entire flat like hundreds of baritone witches. I started to lead the enraged neighbour in the direction of the source of the noise.

Dad limped towards us, grinning like a murderous clown barely visible through the dim light and cannabis smoke. I was now between the neighbour and Dad and we all continued towards the sound. The door of the bathroom was ajar and the volume of the sound became louder. Dad grabbed the bathroom door, turned around to look at the angry neighbour, smiled and presented the scene.

Bartholomew was crouched either side of the bath wearing only a loincloth, with his balls dangling down. Resting between his thighs was a huge didgeridoo. His cheeks were inflated and his eyes were closed, and he seemed to be in a trance. The monotonous, constant noise was amplified by the porcelain bath.

The neighbour hesitated, uncertain how to react, his hammer dropping to his side. The Strangler then appeared in his pink shorts, consuming the last available light and space left in the corridor. The neighbour was trapped in a world only dreamed up in his worst nightmares and, now fully traumatised, froze. Dad leaned into the neighbour and, sensing his vulnerability, squeezed him affectionately on the arm. He whispered, 'You're OK. You're OK.'

Strangler shook his head in disapproval at everyone. The neighbour, realising that he wasn't a threat, then took his chance to manoeuvre past him. As he passed, he looked me directly in the eyes and, knowing that I understood his misery, said, 'Please no more . . . no more.'

He moved out a week later.

10

CROSSING THE LINE

Tring, 1980–4

Life had been very different when we were in Tring. Mum, Jemima and I lived at a much calmer, sedentary pace. I was probably considered an oddity within the averageness of what was expected but we all found our space to fit in. Jemima flourished at her school, which was a world away from the tougher realities of Aylesbury. The Arts Educational School was located in a beautiful manor house, once owned by the Rothschilds, in the centre of the town. Tring Park was their hunting ground and where Walter Rothschild created a huge collection that was later gifted to the Natural History Museum.

Our house was posh enough to have a name, Orchard Cottage. It had an acre of garden with a wooden summer house where I learned to smoke. Part of the house was over two hundred years old, with narrow and awkward spaces and a cellar that had the damp smell of the past. It had two old barns, one that Mum converted into a photographic dark room and the other for our many garden-related machines. Mum had a studio within the house and we bought a piano for the living room. We gradually were lured into a new, slow-paced, all-white world of country people. I began to play rugby, eventually making the local team and ensuring all weekends were booked for Mum and me to travel to other clone villages/towns, like Long Marston or Amersham. Local sports-club culture guaranteed the worst of all humanity, and we were becoming the very folk we were never meant to be. We were comfortable and without problems; we were becoming content.

When Colin and James finally visited, it was shocking how out of place they appeared. Tring simply didn't have Asian families living there then. A local yob who had gushed in admiration of Dad a few days before asked me openly why I was with two Pakis. I was unprepared to deal with the divide as I had no awareness of racism. I wanted Colin and James to disappear so everyone would feel comfortable and in their right place. They came less and less often, and our kaleidoscopic world was swapped for plainer, more ordinary things that cost more money. But everything changed in a momentary lapse of concentration on a cold winter's night.

Mum, Jemima and I were travelling back from Oxford one evening after visiting some friends. Jemima and I were asleep in the back of the new Volvo Dad had just bought us when we were suddenly thrown forward. I found myself on the floor behind the front seat but seemingly OK. A long silence occurred before anything began to make any sense. I pulled myself up and looked around. Jemima had blood all over her face and wasn't moving. Mum appeared motionless. I could see the blurred shapes of other people outside the car. Mum slowly turned her head around and told me calmly to leave.

I opened the door to my right-hand side and

dropped on to a grass bank. A man was lying next to the car perfectly still. Someone had placed a blanket over most of his body. I had no idea what was wrong with him but didn't consider for a moment that he was dead. A motorbike lay on its side a few hundred feet away. It seemed our car had veered from one side of the dual carriageway into the opposite lane of traffic and then into a ditch. Someone was crouching down, talking to Mum through her open window. An elderly couple approached me very cautiously and took my hand. They spoke to me softly and led me away from the man lying on the ground. An ambulance arrived and I got in the back accompanied by the old lady, who continued to hold my hand all the way to the hospital.

At the hospital I waited and waited until Jemima was stretchered past me. I ran to say hello and she sat up and smiled manically, her face still covered in blood. Then she closed her eyes and passed out. Luckily she only had concussion.

It took several hours to release Mum from the front of the Volvo. She had broken her leg and her arm, and her shoulder was shattered. The solidity of the Volvo had probably saved her life but both

Jemima and I were not wearing seatbelts at the time so were incredibly fortunate to be alive. Mum had fallen asleep at the wheel and the car had driven directly into the motorcyclist coming the opposite way, killing him instantly.

The physical recovery for Mum took a long time and she stayed in hospital for many months. Mentally, I doubt she ever recovered as the debt was too unbearable to consider. Jemima and I were young enough for the concept to be too abstract to be painful. I still didn't understand that the man had died and that his family must have held Mum responsible.

Dad sprang into action. He came to live with us in Tring and brought his ex-partner Denise with him. Denise was kind and mothered us and ensured we were OK. I remember clearly the Trinidadian banana bread she made us, which to this day is the best thing I've ever eaten.

After months of operations, Mum learned to walk again. Soon after she left the hospital she went to America to visit her friends and recuperate. She was gone for what seemed an endless amount of time.

Dad hired someone to come and look after us. Dawn was a flower-power nanny with one pair of dungarees and a giant sack of carrots. She was amiable and spacey enough for us to love her company. Dawn sang spiritual songs with her acoustic guitar, had no real rules and acted like Julie Andrews if she'd been on acid. She only ate carrots. The strange diet eventually dyed her skin orange and made her very ill.

A year later, Mum went to court and was charged with manslaughter due to reckless driving. She was given a suspended sentence because of her family circumstances. She tried to explain to us what really happened and how she felt about it. All I remember is calling her a murderer and that was the last we ever mentioned it.

Clothes, Style and Music in London, 1986

Style was an unobtainable mystery as I just didn't have any clothes that I felt represented me. I was fine while I was in Chiswick as it was a cultureless, toxic salmon-pink Pringle jumpers and horrible high-street trousers type of place. Holland Park kids had a different ancestry that was reflected in their fashion and to be expressive was encouraged.

They were already going to nightclubs like the Opera House or the Mud Club where rare grooves and disco was played and everyone wore exuberant second-hand clothing. It wasn't out of the question to go to school in high-heeled boots and a beige safari jacket. But my attempts at fitting in left me looking out of place as I had no sartorial flow. I found a pair of vintage orange and brown velvet flares in the back of Dad's cupboard. They were from Mr Freedom, a shop owned by Tommy Roberts who specialised in pop art fashion in the late sixties. I combined these with an old waistcoat from a 1930s dinner suit and an ill-fitting train driver's hat. It was an experimental look that felt more desperate than natural but I was happy to be free of my provincial choices.

But some kids just understood how to look good no matter what they wore. They usually could dance as well, which was a big thing in the mid-eighties, pre-acid house and techno when movements became more simplified. There was an emphasis on James Brown dancefloor chops that were gymnastically hard to achieve.

Philip Sallon hosted the Mud Club every Friday night. He would sit on his long stall at the entrance to

the Astoria on Charing Cross Road, waiting for someone to disappoint him. We would arrive in a glorious
arrangement of pimped-up clothing and ridiculous
footwear. He would scan each one of us, more
concerned about our look than age. I could never
compete with Zenaide or Karim, a young star of the
dancefloor who was born for the night, but I would
have already guaranteed my entrance by calling the
guest list and pretending to be Dad. Philip would
point his long finger at someone unwanted. They
would inevitably be in a group who were totally
willing to abandon their friend without any consideration as long as they successfully gained entry.

How much I was willing to let go of my inhi-
bitions depended on what drugs I had taken. To
dance felt great but to do it in the company of some
of the more confident kids required bravura – unless
I was high on speed and no longer cared. Then suddenly no one else cared either. The loud music, the
velvet flares, the speed and the partially lit smiles
on your friends' faces meant you were in a place
of total freedom and it felt blissful. And through the
illuminating flashes you would catch a glimpse of
Karim sliding across the floor.

The next morning we would huddle around

someone's bedroom, usually Zenaide's, unable to sleep. The speed that felt so powerful at its peak would let you down in cruel stages of increasing self-doubt. And the memory of the amazing evening would be swapped for total regret until the next weekend.

We started wearing Adidas trainers with fat laces and Volkswagen signs on chains like the Beastie Boys. We would rip them off the front panel of VW Golfs until they stopped making them for this reason. We tried to look tough but mostly looked theatrical and slightly ridiculous. But we had a style that we thought we owned and separated us from the other generations. Hip hop was a growing movement and was still accessible. We saw Run-DMC, Whodini, LL Cool J and the Beastie Boys on the same bill at the Hammersmith Odeon in September 1986, just before the Beasties' debut album *Licensed to Ill* was released.

We bought any records that came out on the Def Jam or Tommy Boy labels. Afrika Bambaataa released *Planet Rock* and by then the Street Sounds Electro series was making its first specifically electro hip-hop compilation albums with rappers like the Real Roxanne, Dr Jekyll and Mr Hyde, and Eric B.

We had various places we could listen to records, including Dad's music room, which had unnecessarily large Tannoy speakers, but the issue was that he could impose his control, with mixed results.

The room had a wall of wooden shelves with all the objects from Dad's travels on display and a collection of art books on Picasso, Goya, Monet and Weegee's photo journalism of Prohibition America. There was a bunch of walking sticks in the corner; one had a guitar built into it, another had a sword hidden in it.

In front of the main windows that looked over the river was a 1969 Slingerland drum kit which had once been owned by Elton John's drummer Nigel Olsson. Its twenty-six-inch bass drum sent a shocking message to the neighbours that no one in this house gave a fuck. Next to the drum kit was a B3 Hammond organ with a Leslie cabinet. It was monstrous and loud, and was the only instrument that competed with the drums.

We would bring our records back there to play as loudly as possible, and then we would go through all of Dad's old funk music like *Look-Ka Py Py* by the Meters, *There's a Riot Goin' On* by Sly and the Family Stone or *The Clones of Funkenstein* by

Parliament. Then we would try and jam on all the instruments. This was when the neighbours really suffered as nothing could have been worse than a loud noise made badly by us.

Jellies in Hammersmith, London, 1986–7

By the time that Strangler and I were living with Dad his music career had been neglected in favour of acting. He featured in a series of poorly made European art films. This gave him access to money and let him rest from the responsibility of being good at something for a while. As much as he cared about acting as a profession he understood his limitations and sort of didn't give a fuck. The relationship with the Blockheads was strained and he was tired of their expectations. And for the last few years the quality of the music he was writing hadn't been comparable to what had made all of them popular originally. But they were a working band that relied on Dad's commitment and he resented that; he knew he could make money elsewhere. As a result, he was bored and drunk a lot of the time, and Strangler and I suffered. In the morning he was

123

grumpy; in the afternoon he was philosophical; by the evening, if he was drinking, he was a cunt.

Strangler and I originated tactics in order to offset Dad's unpredictable behaviour. The night was the real problem because that's when he wanted your time, he wanted you to listen. For the first few beers, he was light-hearted and jovial but if you couldn't escape you were in trouble. It was great for anyone unaccustomed to it as they all thought he was fantastic, they saw Dad's mania as inspiring. But we were weary of the certainty of it turning nasty. He wanted you to get upset as the drama was his real addiction, not the alcohol. The beers were just an excuse to get to that place.

On one particular occasion Strangler and I crossed an ethical line in managing Dad's ever-more extreme mood swings. Strangler suggested we should consider spiking his drink with jellies. Just enough to slow him down and avoid any of the usual confrontation, and he would be none the wiser. Strangler split two of the capsules and emptied the liquid into Dad's drink. There was absolutely no effect for ages as Dad ranted on, demanding our attention, playing Greek folk music and intermittently crying. After an hour, there was just the faintest sign of his eyelids drooping. He tried to stand up and click his calliper into place but he lost his balance, sat back down again and looked a little confused. His facial muscles began to sag, his bottom lip then curled above the top one and his eyes slowly closed. He was out cold, sitting on his favourite chair like a sedated rhinoceros. Strangler picked him up over his shoulder and put him on his bed, making sure his head was turned in the direction of his heart. He undid his boots and left the door open so we could keep an eye on him.

Lisa was a year older than me and had already left Holland Park. She had started a youth training scheme as an assistant hairdresser, which meant she had plenty of spare time so we would hang out a lot in the day. Lisa never talked about her home but I could sense that she hated going back there.

Sometimes Lisa would stay over in Hammersmith as Dad didn't care how old we were or whether she was my girlfriend. We would go swimming at Jenny Pool's, who was the daughter of Dr Kit who had originally treated Dad's polio with a form of aquatic therapy. Dr Kit had passed away since but Jenny now ran the pool, and Dad and her had become great friends. Jenny's house was a haven full of other lost souls who she generally looked after.

The issue was that Lisa was Saul's girlfriend and I was becoming increasingly close to her. The tension grew and eventually Lisa and I had a fleeting moment of closeness that for her was nothing more than a kiss but for me turned everything upside down.

The spectacle I created after this event had little to do with transgression and more to do with how emotionally chaotic I must have been at the time. I purposely let everyone know what had happened. Saul didn't say anything and probably considered it as silly as it was but my despair grew in momentum, which eventually culminated in me swallowing a handful of Strangler's jellies.

I woke up with a doctor slapping me round the face. I had no idea where I was but I could see the foggy outline of Dad with Strangler behind him. Strangler had found me slumped over in his bedroom and had carried me all the way to Charing Cross Hospital. Luckily I didn't need my stomach pumped as the temazepam were relatively harmless. I was allowed to go home the next day. It was the third time I had been to Charing Cross within the year. I'm not sure if anyone ever told my mum and, as usual, no one ever discussed it again.

Chiswick, London, 1986–7

Mum's world was different from Dad's in a lot of positive ways and some not so. Sutton Court was a well-heeled block of mansion flats that overlooked a pretty communal garden just off Sutton Court Lane, which ran through the leafy heart of Chiswick. It was clean and had food in the fridge, light bulbs in the sockets and shower curtains. There was an ice-cream machine and an incinerator that disposed of organic matter. A big, bulky television and a video player. Unstained fitted carpets and the windows were cleaned once a week. Jemima and I had cosy rooms next door to each other and Mum had a lovely big studio.

Mum's studio was a sanctuary of stillness away from some of the unwanted chaos. She painted in watercolour, oil and acrylic or drew in pencil and charcoal. Unlike some of her contemporaries at the Royal College who helped establish the pop art movement in the late 1950s and early 1960s, she was more into the slow arts like her father Thomas, who began painting the docks in Liverpool in the 1920s. Peter Blake, who taught both Mum and Dad at the time that he created the *Sgt Pepper's Lonely Hearts Club Band* front cover for the Beatles, greatly admired Mum's style. But her figurative paintings were never in fashion, unlike Dad's screenprints of Lee Marvin or sequinned glamour girls, which were very much inspired by the era.

Another gloomier ambience was also present in Chiswick. Mum and Clive had a complicated relationship and, as a result, there was always a sense of tension around the house. Clive couldn't always assimilate his tough Cardiff edge into the way we lived. The presence of Dad's influence on us financially was possibly a frustration to him. Mum and Clive would argue sometimes and then they would go off and occupy different parts of the house and drink on their own.

After Jemima completed her time at ballet school she met Phil, who was a dancer at the prestigious Rambert Dance Company. He was confident and exuberant, and probably what Jemima needed to give her some distance away from either side of our uncomfortable family. Phil had an inarguably large mole on the side of his cheek that upset his otherwise symmetrical face. This became his damning feature to our unimpressed dad. Phil's uninhibited, touchy-feely style of communication didn't go down too well with Strangler either, and he openly referred to him as 'The Mole'. Phil didn't take any of it very seriously and remained himself. Eventually Jemima followed Phil to Antwerp to work for Jan Fabre, an established perform-ance artist and modern dance choreographer. Sometimes they would perform naked, covered just in Bic pen illustrations – much to my distress when I was forced to watch.

Mum remained hopeful that I could salvage my education. She was convinced that I had a few organisational syndromes that obstructed my learn-ing. Coupled with the social impact of Dad's fame, she thought there had to be some reason why I found it difficult to be at school. She tried several different methods to trigger my interest. First, she hired Clive's sister, Lynne, who was enthusiastic and tried to find what might wake me up. We briefly bonded over *The Catcher in the Rye* but overall she was no match for my indifference.

Then Mum found a private college called Collingham Tutors that had smaller class sizes and specialised in helping kids pass their exams. It was very expensive but also easy to get into, not like some of the other private schools. I knew I needed structure as the last few months had been close to the edge. I wanted to feel secure, I wanted people around that weren't always fucked, I wanted to learn and I wanted a normal breakfast.

Dad agreed to pay the enormous fees as he had just made lots of money becoming the voice of the new Toshiba commercials. Plus he must have considered my latest foray into danger a step too far, even for his relaxed style of parenting, and recognised I needed a routine. So it was decided that I could still live at the Hammersmith flat, mostly with the Strangler as Dad would be away for much of the year, but I should spend more time with Mum so she could help with my homework and feed me properly.

With both Jemima and I no longer permanent residents, Mum decided to decorate the flat and hired

Paul, Clive's younger brother, to do the job. Paul was slightly homeless looking and unlike Clive and his two sisters had little academic ambition. He wore funny sandals, had long, unconsidered hair and would eat luncheon meat directly from the tin. But he was lovely to me and we got on well, probably because we were pitched at the same level of productivity at that time. But for some reason Strangler hated him and made this very well known.

Strangler now had a habit of visiting Mum to keep her updated on my wellbeing, which was ironic considering he was giving me speed when I wanted it and I had just overdosed on his jellies.

If Paul answered the door, Strangler would growl at him and refuse to say hello. He would walk past him and then be terribly polite to Mum or Clive. Paul would sheepishly remain silent. I'm not sure why Strangler disliked him so much but it wasn't the first time that he had randomly made someone feel miserable and scared.

11

COLLINGHAM

South Kensington, London, 1987–8

Sian was based in a downtrodden Victorian house on the edge of Queen's Gate, next to Hyde Park. Her classroom was in the basement and there was a small stairwell leading back on to the street where she would lurk beyond sight of anyone above and away from the other teachers in the main Collingham Tutors building.

She had a moth-eaten cashmere cardigan draped over her awkward posture, and unwashed, mousy-brown hair flattened against the side of her face.

Her thick lenses magnified the bloodshot capillaries in her wild gaze. She looked like a scholarly zombie rising from a swamp of dead horses. She was nervous, jittery and defensive, uncertain if you would like her.

She offered me a cigarette and I took it. We smoked on the stairwell, attempting to bond. She spoke in short, high-pitched bursts. She told me that I could achieve if I was willing to let her help and that she could manipulate the results to allow me to progress without pressure.

Collingham Tutors was the main crammer college within a group that was designed to help the wealthy and unruly complete their education. It was essentially a large house with a very small number of students in each class. It catered mostly for kids that had fallen foul of the private school system. Some had been sent away to boarding school at such a young age they hadn't developed a normal sense of empathy. Loveless nannies, draughty mansions and parentless half-terms had left them reckless and disjointed.

Mat Poquita was the first student I began to talk

to. He was wearing an impressive fur coat like he was the Czar of Kensington. His face was roundish and kind. He approached me on the stairs and introduced himself quite formally. His effortless slouch and lack of inhibition were intriguing. He was confident and articulate and less edgy than what I expected at that time when meeting someone new. But he was a template of the type of openness that I would slowly grow accustomed to in my new school environment. My prejudice against posh people was changing as I realised how similar I was to some of them. Mat, for instance, had been on a familiar path of upsets that had forced him out of various schools and had a set of chaotic parents that had made questionable choices on his behalf. He had less money than some of his friends openly displayed.

He was a member of Lads London, a loosely organised gang of toffs that had a manifesto of conquering girls and smoking ultra-strong weed. They adapted their names to end in the word 'tree', which was a posh colloquialism for a spliff. Mat would become Mattree, and Sebtree was another prominent member. The Tree Masons, as they were also known, were the least threatening gang I'd come across but they entertained themselves and were a reminder to me of how different this world was.

Mat and I would meet at lunchtime in the Albany, a dimly lit bar, with a snooker table and a serve-the-young-rich-kids policy, at the bottom of a dishevelled hotel. We would share a flask of vodka and try and discuss Aldous Huxley's *The Doors Of Perception*, which neither of us had read. An odd coterie of others would slowly join us. Theo was older, taller and more sinister than the rest. He had been at the college for a few years as he repeatedly failed his A levels but someone rich and distant paid for him to continue. He had blue hair and hollow eyes, and led a small group of friends into extreme drug taking. He was always accompanied by Sofia, a wholesome and beautiful Italian girl who seemed indifferent to his dark persona. Finn was his cherub-faced lieutenant who was capable of every extreme and had been thrown out of a succession of different boarding schools. And sometimes Theo would be with an anonymous, creepy, older man who was maybe in his early thirties and didn't say much. The man only drank snakebite and black, a combination of lager and cider with a dash of blackcurrant cordial.

I quickly learned my lesson not to overvalue my common-sounding accent and its influence on those I thought were scared of it. For the first few months, I exaggerated my vowels to establish who I wanted to be. It took only one irritated column of poshness to question my credentials as a fighter. I was never a great fighter. I was potentially very good at starting fights but most of my aggression was just gesticulation, a defensive act to repel anyone before any contact. I snarled and screamed and had a convincing stream of invective that usually worked. If it didn't, I was in trouble.

So, after my rehearsed series of insults fell silently on this one opulent rugger-whopper, I knew I was fucked. He grabbed me around the neck like Darth Vader and politely warned me that I'd overstepped the mark. He pawed with me at first, slapping me round the face and chuckling to himself, and then delivered a series of devastating punches that sent me crashing to the floor. He was ready and waiting for me to fall into his trap. He'd been sent to boarding school from the age of seven and left to grow angry, strong and in control of his emotions. These kids were like Spartans.

I told Strangler, who initially thought it was funny

and then considered he should act. He thought better of it, knowing his position was under scrutiny ever since I'd stolen his sleeping pills.

Ferdie was a buoyant character, irrepressibly funny and upbeat, and very popular among my strange assortment of new friends. Felix, his older brother, was less definable. He was more elegant and peculiar but very smart. We and a few others formed a clique that made this new school an enjoyable place to be. The lessons faded in importance and we sorted out different ways of entertaining ourselves.

Addie was an American student who lived locally with her ambiguously absent father. Their house was an impressive structure with an assortment of sexualised *objets d'art* dotted around each floor. At the very top was a cushioned hedonism room with giant ashtrays and a beautiful art deco drinks cabinet. Amid all the splendour was a wooden box in which Addie's father openly kept his week's choice of narcotics. There were always different types of marijuana that we were obliged to steal and sometimes there was cocaine. Coke was still a big leap for us as it had such scary connotations of crack back then, but we still did it.

One day we discovered some pills that had an

oval shape inscribed on each one. We assumed that they were a type of prescription high and probably pretty harmless. It was lunchtime so Ferdie and I took a half each, speculating this would have little effect, and went back to our lessons.

I sat in a biology lesson with three other pupils, unable to concentrate as usual as the teacher droned on enthusiastically about something. A sudden drop in my awareness occurred, as if a second of my time had been stolen. I sat upright, attempting to re-establish my balance. Then multiple waves of irregular feelings came at me and I was finding it difficult to cope.

I said something that I thought sounded normal: 'Ma'am, nausea is a problem for me, you may remember.' I didn't wait for a response. I just needed freedom and confidently walked out.

I was on the top landing of the grand house. It would be break time soon and everyone would gather in the common room at the very bottom. The rushes, some bigger than others, were now coming consistently as I tentatively walked down the stairs. Then there was an almighty crash, like the engine of a Boeing jet had fallen on me from nowhere. The forebidding paintings that decorated each set of stairs felt like they were winking at me.

I reached the empty common room, collapsed and lay still. A familiar accent startled me. Ferdie looked broken. He had fled from his lesson in a similar panic. Whatever poison we had taken without any consideration was now refurnishing our minds. A sudden stampede of students flooded the common-room area for their ten-minute break.

Ferdie and I were now cowering in the corner, desperately trying to reorganise our thoughts. The waves became so intense that we both fell silent. The other pupils surrounded us, intrigued by how pathetic we looked.

Without warning a thousand horizons opened up in my mind and the world changed. I reached out for Ferdie's hand and held it tight. He didn't recoil as it seemed natural to be close right now. A surge of human warmth and understanding covered me and I stood up and smiled at all the other lovely people that had arrived.

'Ferd, man,' I said very earnestly, 'I fucking love you, man.'

'Yeah I know, man.'

Never have I felt such a complete sense of wellbeing.

We intermingled with everyone like missionaries.

The switch was so swift from fear to completeness and understanding that I had no sense of the previous forty minutes. I had arrived and I had purpose, and it was fucking great.

Ferdie and I went to Crazy Larry's that night. It was a small club in Chelsea full of young, aimless society kids. The club's promoter was Robert Pereno, an orange man who wore a biker jacket and cowboy boots. He was a celebrated playboy who preyed on rich girls. We walked around like happy survivors of a plane crash, massaging each other's shoulders and buying everyone drinks. Lads London danced in unison to Public Enemy's 'Yo! Bum Rush the Show'.

That evening I headed back to Mum's as I had a strong urge to be with my family. The drugs had settled into a manageable euphoria and I felt pretty good. Jemima was back from Antwerp and was sitting with Mum and Clive watching television in the front room. I stood at the door and just smiled at them and tried not to talk. Then I said, 'I love you ... a real lot.' I quickly withdrew, knowing I was glowing with narcotics.

*

Dad had been gone for a few months by then and strangely Strangler and I had found peace in some sort of routine.

Every morning Strangler drove me to school in the white Nissan, and would wait outside and make a point of waving at me to frighten the other students. Usually when I returned from school Strangler would cook – or at least he did for the first few months.

He had a set post-war menu: mashed potatoes, meat pie and some sort of vegetable drowned in cheap gravy. After dinner, Strangler would begin his ascent into the night. Because he was a drug dealer of sorts and a member of a night community, he was obliged to be out four to five evenings a week.

Before his ritual began he would prepare all the drugs he needed for that night. He would start by cutting up magazine pages into wraps and then use a vintage set of scales to weigh out different sizes. He would sniff a few lines and then start growling. Then the robing process would start.

Each earring was considered, each turquoise arm bracelet thought about. He had an entangled mesh of chains from which he would carefully pick: maybe the one with an original SS officer's badge, or the one with the customised silver snorting tube. He'd douse himself in a fake cologne and use a can of hairspray to prop up his autumn-red bouffant. Lynyrd Skynyrd was his choice of motivational music and, as the speed kicked in, he would start to retch and sing. He would repeat his stories about the loss of great friends in suspicious circumstances, telling me that 'Pete shouldn't have gone, man, they took him down, man, they ran him down.'

At five in the morning he would loom over my chaise longue, pretending to check if I was asleep. Considering my bed was in the front room sleep was pretty much impossible. Then he would fake a look of surprise that I had woken up and take the opportunity to introduce me to all the empty souls that had followed him back.

It was the smell that haunted me most: the cheap stench of bad living. Jack Daniel's, obnoxious perfume, sulphate, PVC. These were the night chancers, people sold on the idea that wearing eroticised plastic clothes and taking speed somehow defined them as something.

Tricksy was an exception. She was found, perfectly coiled like a serpent goddess, next to my bed.

As my blurry eyes separated the different unknown shapes she was suddenly in full frame, staring directly at me. She had black-painted circles around her eyes and her knee-length blonde hair was spread across the floor. She said absolutely nothing.

Strangler, slugging from a bottle of vodka, paced around her as though she was his captive. Some of the other ornamental goths shuffled around them. They had just been to Slimelight and a fight had broken out. Strangler's face was covered in blood, I'm not sure whose.

'This is Tricksy, Tricksy, oooooooooooah,' Strangler hollered like a crazed sheriff.

Tricksy remained totally silent and unflustered. I was now upright in my chaise longue, still transfixed by her, our gazes locked. She reclined back on both elbows, stretching her endlessly long legs into the middle of the room. She was Cleopatra, at least for the moment, and she made all the hell of this situation bearable. I remained as still as possible, hoping the others would lose interest in me.

Tricksy stood up, unravelling her full potential, and spoke for the first time. 'Stranglerdoro, Stranglerdoro, play the "Hurricane".' Her squeaky pitch betrayed my first impression of her.

'Stranglerdoro' had the tape recorder already in position. The opening bars to Bob Dylan's 'Hurricane' were struggling to come out of the tiny stereo. Tricksy was now animated, arms thrashing randomly, her legs making uncoordinated leaps around the front room. Strangler was circling around her like someone in *The Wicker Man*. The other goths were contributing with irregular movements, the whole room ablaze with motion. I sank back into the bed and just waited.

Strangler still managed to take me to school in the morning – without having had any sleep and with Tricksy singing in the back of the car.

Apart from all the predictable behaviour there was one teacher that broke through. Sian, the teacher who had given me a cigarette in the stairwell and told me she could help me, lured everyone in eventually. She was so completely unorthodox and strange that she was impossible to ignore. She was passionate about what she wanted to teach and she didn't care about any of the protocol on how to achieve her goals. She established a certain level of freedom within the class that bought the pupils' trust. We could smoke inside if we wanted to and she would even provide cigarettes. This suited most of us perfectly but upset a minority of the straighter kids who were there to actually do their exams. But she didn't care so much for them as she wanted the challenge of converting lost children like me. She wanted to prove that English literature was exciting and that she could find some hope in anyone. And for the first time I started to respond.

The new GCSE exam that was to replace the O level in 1988 was based on three modular stages, each one contributing to an overall grade. She decided that I needed so much groundwork to make up for the years of lost schooling that she should cheat the first round. This would give me space to breathe and encouraged me to think that she was on my side.

Strangler was so impressed by Sian, especially that she let me smoke in the class, that he would always pick me up from her lesson and try to talk to her. He would arrive outside the school, slam down his horn and she would go to greet him almost coquettishly. They would witter on, discussing my progress. They had the most unlikely admiration for each other.

Over the course of a few months my enthusiasm started to dip. I wasn't prepared to give the commitment that Sian needed from me. I was too undisciplined and, in reality, living with the Sulphate Strangler meant I was residing with a hulk of unpredictably. I started to flake on everything and no one accounted for where I was or what I was doing. My new friends had money, houses, cars, booze, drugs and endless amounts of time: I had found the ultimate spring of chaos and it was fantastic.

One morning I took some magic mushrooms before going to Sian's lesson. I sat down and opened my textbook, and had no idea where I was. The uptight Greek girl opposite stared at me with a mixture of concern and disgust. Sian's over-expressive posturing was starting to make me laugh. Her face was like a melted wheelie bin. I started to draw oversized letters, unconnected to anything that she was saying, on each page of the book. I knew that I had to contain myself so I awkwardly stood up and left. I never returned to her class.

Collingham was reluctant to expel anyone as it prided itself on helping people like me and relied on everyone's enormous fees. A confrontation with the art teacher on an earthquake simulation machine in the Natural History Museum made them consider it. Mr Ferris was a youngish, over-motivated teacher and, to my mind, not very good. I was a little irked that he didn't recognise my potential because, at this stage, I was still considering going to art school as both sides of my family had been to a reputable one in the past.

On the class outing, I had led a small party of pupils away from the given brief to sketch fossilised whalebones. We smoked a spliff, got suitably stoned and headed to the earthquake machine. We spent an hour tipping it from side to side to the frustration of the museum staff. Out of nowhere, the art teacher ran at me, grabbed me by the lapels of my coat and dragged me off the machine. The noise of the spectacle was amplified by the echoey marble corridor of the Victorian building. When a small crowd of tourists gathered around us, Mr Ferris released his hold, suddenly aware of his actions. I never returned to his lesson.

The common room at Collingham had become a bartering ground for anything we wanted. Theo and his group were getting into opioids and lots of coke. We were taking speed, as I had an endless supply of it, which we now consumed with jellies to make it more interesting, one taking the edge off the other and eventually allowing you to sleep. Sometimes we would just take the jellies, which I now knew were relatively harmless. We would take three or four at a time, drink a couple of pints and then slap each other round the face without feeling any pain. We'd find this hilarious.

Strangler wouldn't always give me the drugs but I knew where he stored them and, if I was brave enough, I would just take them, but this was at considerable risk. If he went out, he would leave a small piece of tape at the bottom of the door to indicate if anyone had entered his room. He kept his drugs in a primitive metal safe with a rudimentary lock, which I could easily pick. Then I had to decide which bag to take from as there were usually several different colours, including some reddish and others pure white.

This meant people started to pester me at school to get them drugs. In an act of meanness I sold an awkwardly posh kid a lump of mud, pretending it was hash, and was caught red-handed by the teacher patrolling the common room. I was immediately taken to the headmaster's office. Technically, I hadn't sold any drugs but I was still kicked out of Collingham.

12

BURNING BEDS AND CRASHING CARS

West Kensington, London, 1988

Ferdie moved into a flat with Finn opposite the Olympia exhibition centre. Above an old bakery, it had two floors and shared a bathroom with the flat below. Ferdie lived at the very top with a sparse arrangement of furniture and a soiled mattress. I spent almost every moment at this flat as, yet again, I had nothing to do.

After a few months it was decided that I should

move in as well and share Ferdie's room. I started by bringing over my crate of rare records and a meagre assortment of clothes. We placed another bed next to Ferdie's, like it was a dormitory, and that night we spent the last of our money on the only cheap alcohol we could afford in celebration. We smoked a few spliffs and became hungry and cold. The flat had no insulation and only one temperamental electric heater. At one in the morning we decided to walk the three miles back to my mum's in Chiswick for warmth and food. We snuck into the flat, ate as much as we could find and went to sleep in my old room.

Mum, surprised that we were there, woke us up the next morning and said Finn was on the phone and urgently needed to speak to Ferdie. After a few minutes he came back into the room and said we had to go right now. We scrambled to put on our clothes and ran to catch a bus back to Olympia.

There were several fire engines lining the street outside the flat. The windows from the top room were blown out. Finn's room was relatively untouched except for the water damage from the fire hoses, but ours was totally destroyed. My bed had disappeared completely and the crate of rare records had melted to the floor. Strangely, a pair of my toxic silver trousers had morphed into an eerie shape due to the material and were standing up on their own.

It was never proven how the fire started but we suspected it was due to a fault in the electric heater. The landlords suggested it was a discarded cigarette but had no interest in pursuing the matter.

Hamburg, 1988

I was now back between Mum and Dad's, neither of which was ideal for me or them. Mum and Clive were fighting and I wasn't helping by being around. Dad had started to tire of living with the Strangler, and his reasons for being at the Hammersmith flat hadn't really worked out considering I had been thrown out of school.

To ease the tension, Dad decided to invite Strangler and me to help him on a trip to Hamburg to film *Burning Beds*, another low budget art film. It gave me something to do since I was no longer at Collingham and Strangler could reconnect with some old friends, Hamburg being a playground of his touring days.

As we began our descent into Hamburg airport, Strangler made the sound of a Lancaster bomber to the disgust of everyone on the plane. I knew then that this trip was doomed.

Dad was melancholic and Strangler seemed more jittery than usual, and there was a lot of tension between them.

We arrived in the centre of town and dropped Strangler off at a dishevelled hotel in the Reeperbahn. We then travelled the short distance to the Four Seasons, where Dad and I both had nice rooms.

We met a few hours later for dinner in the hotel restaurant. Dad was uncharacteristically subdued as we ate our food in silence, and then my sense of unease grew as he started to drink.

Strangler was in his full sparkling night costume and stank of a putrid cologne. His finest jewellery had been carefully organised to show his prize pieces with the SS badge openly on display. He was excitable in anticipation of seeing his great old friend, Heinrich.

The elderly waiter approached us cautiously to clear our plates, and Dad grabbed hold of his wrist when he attempted to take his almost empty glass of beer away. The waiter recoiled, shook his head and left with our dirty plates still on the table.

Strangler started to talk very loudly about Heinrich to lighten the atmosphere, but Dad wasn't listening. Strangler's mood darkened and he began criticising the Durys and how we would never know what steerage class really felt like even though both of us pretended to be working class. He said it was disgusting that we were in the Four Seasons but were perfectly willing to let their beast servant live in shit.

Dad just said, 'U-boat,' under his breath, then very loudly, 'Fucking U-boat. If he's that old, he's responsible,' putting an end to Strangler's rant.

'What, Ian?' said Strangler.

'He fucking survived the war, that waiter cunt,' Dad said with full menace.

'Not now, Ian, that's really not kind, man,' said Strangler, even though he'd recently been enjoying mimicking the noise of an aerial bombing.

The waiter swooped in for a second attempt at clearing our plates without saying anything. Dad looked at him now with drunken eyes following his every move.

'Do you think I wasn't there, man?' Dad said, reaching out again to grab the waiter's hand.

The waiter stared sternly into Dad's eyes. 'I refuse to be hurt by your suggestions or by this animal. We will not tolerate any problems.'

Dad leaned into Strangler, affectionately resting his head on his giant arms. Smiling, he said, 'Mr Fucking Animal, whack him.'

Strangler ignored both Dad and the waiter, and looked at me, choosing to pretend that none of this was happening.

We both knew that responding to Dad's indifference to upsetting people only encouraged him, while it usually expired when he was ignored.

The waiter was now talking to the rest of the restaurant staff and they were clearly discussing what to do next. The corners of all the other diners' eyes were concentrated on us. Dad repeated his command to Strangler to hit someone. Strangler, realising the situation was getting out of control, stood up and said, 'Ian, not this time.' He walked out.

Dad stood up unsteadily, clicked his calliper into place and pulled out as much money as he could find. He scattered it over the table disrespectfully. He then asked me to escort him out of the restaurant, insisting we walk through the middle. We slowly manoeuvred ourselves through the other tables towards the lift. Everyone gawped in disbelief at the small limping man with his enormous head being assisted by his spotty son. As we passed, the waiter stood still with his chin held high while his colleagues shook their heads slowly.

Dad grinned to himself and said, 'Auschwitz, that's all you got.'

We made it to the lift. As the lift doors closed it seemed to seal the whole incident shut.

'We're up early tomorrow, Bax, so get an alarm call from the front desk.'

When we reached our floor he whistled off towards his room without a suggestion of what had just happened.

Tobias, the production assistant on *Burning Beds*, picked us up in a huge Mercedes at 7 a.m. the next morning to drive us towards the harbour. With a warm smile, he turned round to us and said that the hotel was concerned that it wasn't the right place for us to stay but that he had found a lovely apartment closer to the location.

After a long day's filming and some wooden acting from Dad on an unstable ship, we were taken to our new place, which was rudimentary and clean.

Strangler, who had been out all night, arrived later on that evening and decided he would stay as well, claiming his hotel was uninhabitable. I would now sleep on the sofa in the front room.

The uncomfortable feeling brewing among all three of us was getting worse. Dad was a disillusioned singer doing another awful film that he plainly didn't believe in. Strangler was a hopeless drug addict uncertain of where he was going to live. And I was sixteen, unschooled, spotty and without any plan whatsoever.

That evening Strangler disappeared back into Hamburg's sleazy night. Dad and I got into a huge argument about my future and what he said was my total lack of respect for anything. We shouted and screamed so loudly that the neighbours started banging on the walls. Dad responded by smashing his plate on to the floor so I threw mine as well. He then opened a kitchen cabinet and swept all the glasses out, creating a horrible din. We broke everything we could find in a frenzied moment of destruction. Then he began to cry and tell me how much he loved me and how amazing I was. We had a long hug and left the thick sea of debris that now covered the kitchen floor for someone else to clean up.

Tobias picked us up at seven on the dot, as expected. This time his face looked less pleased. He waited for a while before he built up the courage to tell us that we would have to move again. Dad smiled triumphantly.

I wanted to go home and Dad agreed that, after all the drama, it was probably the right thing to do, so that night I got a flight back.

When I arrived at Heathrow I was stopped by the customs officer, who took me aside to inspect my bag. Under my clothes was an assortment of discarded jellies that I had carelessly forgotten about. These were mixed up with a leaking tube of skin-tone foundation that I used to cover up my increasingly spotty face. Its beige, powdery consistency had started to dry and was worrying the customs officer. I was transferred to another room. They asked how I was travelling on a BA business-class flight at the age of sixteen. Eventually, after hours of trying to contact my parents and having identified the make-up, they let me go.

After a few months of exhausting everyone's patience hopping between houses, Mum asked me to get a job. Luckily my friends, including Felix, were dropping out of school so the two of us decided to go job hunting together – or we convinced our- selves that's what we were going to do. He picked me up from Chiswick in a disgustingly coloured light green Vauxhall, his stepdad's new car. Finn was in the back for no reason, his kindly face masking a thousand devious intentions. Felix turned the car around, exited Sutton Court and then randomly sped up. He drove at a large pile of sand placed outside some scaffolding and the car flew into the air. It crashed down on to its fragile frame and readjusted itself back into the centre of the road. Finn's whispery laughter and Felix's cold grin lit up the car. There was no mention of job hunting again as we leapt over a small bridge, smashing the car's undercarriage against the curved road.

We arrived at an empty clearing next to the Thames where Felix slammed the handbrake on and spun the car full circle. We spent a few moments skidding in the dust. He then directed the car at great speed down a pedestrian pathway that ran alongside the river. At first the path was wide enough for the Vauxhall, but the incline of the slope towards the water increased as the path narrowed and the car was soon sliding towards the Thames. Felix accelerated to maintain our balance. To the left was a thick wall of shrubbery and to our right was a sheer drop into the river.

After a third of a mile at terrifying speed, we started to slip back towards the river so Felix swung the car up the hill, heading for a cluster of trees that had now replaced the thick shrubbery. The bonnet clipped the first tree and the car was flipped into the air. It crashed back down on to its roof and started to roll down towards the river. After two revolutions the car miraculously smashed into a twelve-inch-thick concrete fence, which only ran along that particular tiny stretch of the bank. The car lifted up but was caught on a horizontal steel pole that ran between two concrete pillars. The car now dangled less than half a foot above the raging river.

I was suspended upside down, silently staring at the torrent below my head, still uncertain if we would survive.

Felix's first instincts were to claim his cigarettes, which had fallen below his head. Even while upside down above the River Thames, he remained unflustered. He calmly unclipped his seatbelt, lowered himself down and climbed out through the partially open window on his side.

Finn started to panic and, worried the car was about to roll over into the water or explode, began kicking the back window. Felix shouted at him to pull himself together and then dusted himself down. The rear doors were buckled shut. I unclipped my belt and tumbled on to the crumpled roof. The car tipped at an angle away from the river and I barely squeezed through the available gap. Finn wriggled between the two front seats and Felix bent down and helped ease him out. Felix was now enjoying being the hero of the disaster he had created. We stood in awe of what we had achieved. There was an eerie silence around us: no sirens or worried members of the public clambering to our rescue. We had crashed into the unused grounds of a new health club.

Felix made the clever assumption that if the gym was open it would be full of strong men that could lift the car back on to its correct side. He went off to investigate and came back with four bemused weightlifters.

Suddenly from every angle the police arrived, in vans, cars and by foot. They took us off individually and strip-searched us. They found a couple of jellies and some used Rizlas on me, but surprisingly nothing on the others. When they learned that our names were Felix, Finn and Baxter, they decided that we were just three soppy middle-class kids that had taken the wrong turning. A kindly policeman explained that we would have certainly died if we had hit the river roof-first. Then we were released without any further action.

The police dropped us in Baker Street, where Felix's parents lived. John, Felix's stepfather, took us for a pizza. He was concerned about our ordeal but totally unbothered about his new car being written off. We proudly retold the story, each from our own perspective.

As the pizzas were served, we saw a tow truck taking the light green Vauxhall past the window. Its roof was caved in and its front lights were smashed. It was an ugly reminder of how lucky we'd been. We ate in silence.

13

INDEPENDENCE

Chiswick and Hammersmith, 1988

Felix wrote to me from Long Island and told me how desperately unhappy he was. Since the crash the whole family had uprooted to America after John, his stepfather, had been given a well-paid post as a philosophy lecturer at Adelphi University, New York state.

His brother Ferdie was faring better in the new world but Felix's brand of individualism was at odds with the uncompromisingly macho environment, plus he'd pissed off some dangerous drug dealers.

I responded to Felix and told him in no uncertain terms that he was always welcome to come and live with me. He wrote back immediately, without consideration, and told me the date he was arriving. I picked him up at the airport and tried to explain that things were a little up in the air and we might have to adapt, contrary to the original offer. The first place we would go to was Mum's as I knew she and Clive had gone way to France for the weekend. I didn't tell Felix that I was banned from the house if either Mum or Clive weren't there.

Dad had been away for months so I was staying with the Strangler but life with him had become more and more erratic. I was at the mercy of his huge mood swings, depending on his sleep patterns. Strangler would stay up for three days selling drugs, at which point a chemical sheen of perspiration would shimmer over his orange skin, then he would take thirty jellies and recover for two days. He would appear mid-hibernation and march along the corridor towards the bathroom, a sweat-drenched sleeping mask around his forehead, wearing only his tiny silk boxer shorts. He was a colossal mound of reflexes unaware of his surroundings. I would attempt to talk to him but his eyes would glaze over. He would take a huge gulp of the cheapest supermarket cola and then piss like a horse. It was a difficult cycle to live with.

Felix and I settled into my mum's well-stocked house – we smoked pot, ate everything we could find and then went into the night to reacquaint him with his old haunts.

We returned early on Sunday morning, knowing Mum and Clive would be back soon, so I could try and cover our tracks.

We both fell asleep and were woken up by Clive powering through the front door in the afternoon. I was on the sofa in the front room and Felix was hidden away in my bedroom. Mum came and spoke to me in her soft, understanding tone, at first trying to placate me. I vaguely listened while waking up from my deep slumber. When she tried to get my attention more directly, I snapped back at her and told her to shut up. I grabbed her coffee cup and threw it against the ceiling.

Mum broke down in tears and Clive rushed in like a South African prison guard. I walked nonchalantly back down the hall towards my room, where Felix was still hiding. As I began to open my door and acknowledged Felix's frightened eyes, Clive spun me round and poked his index finger into my ribcage.

Clive's contorted face shouted 'Your mother does not fucking need this, BAXTER, not fucking at all,' over and over again, showering me in spittle. I looked over to the partially open bedroom door and could see Felix's face staring back at mine. His hand was gesturing for me not to say anything back and prolong this any more.

Clive's rage reduced itself to a simmering contemplation. I walked past him back into the bedroom where Felix had his bags already packed. He whispered in a frightened voice, 'Please, let's just go now.' We left without saying goodbye. We walked to Chiswick High Road and jumped on the bus, and ten minutes later we arrived in Hammersmith. The enormity of Strangler's being was so overwhelming that his day stench could be smelled from down the street. A sense of decay – like an abandoned abattoir – lingered as we approached the front door. I undid the multiple locks tentatively. It was early evening and we had no idea what to expect. Strangler lived in a heightened state of fear.

It was eerily quiet as we entered the darkened

hallway. The outside light bounced off the empty vodka bottles strewn across the floor, and Tricksy's knee-length PVC boots were discarded on top of my chaise longue. The kitchen had been ransacked, a knife left in a tub of melted margarine and stale bread spread across the surfaces, but there was no noise. Just the smell of chemical sweat and tobacco.

Felix and I sat with uncertainty on my daybed and contemplated what had just happened. Only through the eyes of someone else impartial to your desensitised cycle of craziness do you gain perspective. We hadn't spoken much up to this point. He began to adjust to the realities of his new surroundings. All comfort had vanished and we were now in the lair of the beast.

I heard Strangler's door creak as he pushed open his barricade. Every pillow and blanket had been placed around the gaps in his bedroom door to prevent any uninvited light. A few growls proceeded.

'Bax, is that you? Bax, you cunt!'

I jumped up, knowing something was wrong, and to spare Felix from another confrontation attempted to pre-empt him reaching us.

The memory was suddenly very clear. Three days earlier I had taken the laundrette money left on the hatch. Amid all the madness, drugs and disappointment this was considered, in Strangler's warped logic, a massive injustice. I immediately switched direction and began to run towards the other end of the flat. He stopped and looked at Felix. 'What the fuck you looking at?'

I couldn't run any further and turned to confront him. He lunged towards me. 'The fucking money, you cunt, you fucking little cunt!' His right arm stretched out and grabbed me by the throat and he lifted me off the floor. The last available air bled out of my mouth and, as my legs dangled and my eyes filled with water, I managed to whisper, 'Strangler, Strangler.'

He looked straight through me, seemingly unable to connect with the wrong he was committing. In the grip of death I thought about Felix and all the inconvenience he was suffering. Slowly, Strangler lowered me back down to the floor and released his murderous hand from my neck. He turned around, walked calmly to the kitchen and made a monstrous gulping noise. His neurological pathways were so broken that he was unable to concentrate on one task for long and even his rage could be interrupted by sudden thirst.

I inhaled as much air as possible and crept down the corridor. I found Felix frozen just as I'd left him. He must have considered for a moment what my fate had been. This wasn't Clive, a frustrated computer engineer from Cardiff, this was the Sulphate Strangler, a six-foot-seven, drug-addled, professionally violent man.

We quickly gathered our belongings together as quietly as possible so as not to remind Strangler of our presence. He made some heavy breathing noises. We tiptoed out of the flat and into the night without a plan.

Felix and I headed for the only place we knew we could sleep. Julian was a trainee doctor and the brother of one of our good friends. He was generous, older, and with a flat of his own in Battersea. He allowed us to stay on a tiny sofa and an uncarpeted floor. We spent the next few nights repeating the story of the violence I had encountered in both of my parents' homes. And then the reality of the helpless situation dawned on me: I was sixteen, had no money and nowhere to live, and I'd never worked in my life.

Galloway Road, London, 1988

Felix and I fictionalised our qualifications and scoured the job listing sections of all the newspapers in search of appropriate employers. Julian lent me an ill-fitting suit and Felix wore his favourite peppermint green three-piece with pleated trousers.

Within a week, I had a job with a new chain of shops specialising in the then very fashionable Swatch Watch. I would start at the AM:PM packing department where I would learn the company ethos and nature of its products. Felix, meanwhile, convinced a firm of City speculators to employ him as a trainee broker.

We approached a friend from Collingham whose father had recently been disbarred as a judge on corruption charges. We knew he had several run-down properties in west London that he was under pressure to rent out.

Thirty-five Galloway Road, one of the grimmest back streets of Shepherd's Bush, was now our new home. One mighty weed grew from the loosely paved garden where a constant stream of water poured from a faulty overflow tank. The kitchen was a narrow afterthought awkwardly placed in the middle of a connecting corridor. The whole house was haunted by years of bad living that had soaked through the walls and Formica, creating an unremovable bleakness. The putrid carpet was trodden with the dust and dead skin of a thousand forgotten souls. But the house was ours and we were free, sort of.

We divided the house between us. Felix took over the upstairs and I would sleep in the front room accompanied by the constant hum of the television as my brain was so wounded by Strangler drugs.

Felix's grandparents delivered a generous vanload of bygone furniture that had lain in storage for over thirty years. Among the vintage haul of an assortment of uncomfortable chairs, forebidding mirrors and dainty coffee tables was his grandad's medicine cabinet stocked with pre-war opium and amphetamines. Felix was obliged to consume them all.

I started work in the AM:PM offices where we had to endlessly apply magnetic strips to the Swatch Watch packaging in the guise of learning about the product. After a week of repeating the same action I was sent to the flagship store that proudly sat on the front of the newly built Plaza shopping centre in the middle of Oxford Street.

Asif was the store manager as he was slightly older and claimed he had experience in retail, but there was little evidence of this in practice. He had hired his friend Darren, who was less concerned about his lack of capabilities, as his assistant. The three of us would congregate in the tiny stock room that doubled as Asif's office. He would make the less favoured staff do all the menial jobs and we would just smoke pot.

One morning while cleaning up the stock room, I accidentally smashed a bottle of white spirit over the nylon carpet. I half-heartedly attempted to clean it up but was distracted when both Asif and Darren clambered in to smoke a joint before the shop opened. I took the last drag and flicked the roach on to the carpet without any consideration. A blue flame mushroomed into the centre of the room and then travelled along the floor like magic. A deep chemical blackness rose from the melting carpet and lifted itself into every corner. In a choreographed sequence, the sprinklers on the shop floor released a monsoon of water in every conceivable direction. Instantly a river of debris formed in between each aisle, snatching anything in its way.

Asif screamed at us to save the stock. We grabbed

what we could and started piling it into a corner. I found Darren in the stock room stuffing the watches under his jumper. He looked at me and smiled, and pleaded with me to be quiet. I grabbed as many watches as I could, put them under my suit jacket and left the shop.

The Plaza foyer was in total chaos as every sprinkler in every shop had been triggered. A huge wave of water cascaded down the central staircase. I reached the toilets on the second floor, stripped the watches from their packaging and lay them across the top of the cisterns. I discarded the boxes out the window and ran back down to the shop.

I could see a herd of fire engines parked outside the Plaza doors. The water was so constant that Oxford Street itself had started to flood. When I entered the shop, the staff were on their knees desperately trying to save anything floating in the reservoir. Asif looked broken and was just staring at the stock room. Two company bosses had arrived from head office and were splashing around ineffectively.

'Where have you been? ... Where's Darren?' I didn't really know what to say but Asif suddenly spoke again. 'He's gone, the fucker's gone.'

Darren had decided to scarper with as much stock as possible and conveniently diverted all the attention away from me. Eventually, the authorities had to close down Oxford Street. I stayed until two in the morning, helping the fire brigade and the other AM:PM staff sweep out the water with giant brooms. The next day I was sent to the Carnaby Street branch where I was promoted to assistant manager. The police arrested Darren.

Felix and I braved the bitter winter. Sometimes we would fight first thing in the morning depending on who needed to get to work the earliest. Felix was always well groomed and took pride in his suit being pressed and his shirts being ironed. I slept in the front room so was woken up by him getting ready and I unfairly lashed out a few times.

No matter how you lit the house, the depth of its horrid colouring was hard to reverse. It had an oppressive, ambient gloom. The old furniture and the glow from a dangerous convection heater contributed to its dourness. The central heating had broken down and it became too cold to even bathe.

Eventually we neglected everything, starting

with the kitchen as we failed to wash the plates. These piled up and made it a no-go zone. On one occasion it got so bad we used the bath to wash the dishes as there were so many. From then on we only ate from the local chip shop to avoid any more washing up.

The unused dining room started to fill with clutter. A mound of rubbish developed, including pornographic magazines and uncooked chicken thighs that had gone rancid. After six months it became another no-go zone. Then we realised that we were losing control.

We were cold, poor and deeply unhygienic, and I wanted to go home. I hadn't spoken to either parent for months. I had lost my job as I found it too cold to go to work and was eking out the last of my wages.

Mum called me out of the blue to see if I was OK, and then asked if I wanted to come home. The next day she appeared while Felix was at work and I filled her car with my tattered belongings.

Chiswick, 1989

Mum's was a paradise of clean sheets and warmth for the first month before old tensions crept back in, exacerbated by me lurking around the house.

I needed to find something to do but the discomfort of working in the real world over the last few months had made me reconsider what that might be. I eventually persuaded Dad to send me back to a new tutorial college, close to Collingham, for another attempt at my GCSEs. He agreed on the peculiar stipulation that I study German.

I was now seventeen and I applied every effort during my first few months at Mander Portman Woodward, my new school, and for a brief moment there was a sense of peace. I pretended to enjoy German and generally kept out of trouble. Mum was pleased that I was living back with her and, as I was convincing everyone that I was working hard, we all got along. I'd even received a postcard from Strangler, who after having a huge row with Dad had taken the Nissan and driven to Hamburg, and was now living with Heinrich. He didn't mention strangling me the last time we saw each other but I doubt he even remembered.

I found it hard to make friends at school as there was something different about it compared to Collingham, which had basically been full of mercenaries like me. These were glossy rich kids that I couldn't relate to. So on my lunch breaks I would hang out with Molly. She had recently moved to London to go to Queen's College, a snooty school for girls on Harley Street. We'd been introduced through Julian, the junior doctor, who'd asked me to look out for her. Her stepfather was a wealthy asparagus farmer from Lincolnshire and she was well provided for with a brand new VW Golf and a rented flat on Gloucester Road, right next to my school.

On one particular lunch break, and led by her initiative, we went to her flat and progressed to being more than just friends. Afterwards I joyously ran to the Albany pub to try and share my news, only to find Theo, the last remaining pupil from the golden Collingham era. I realised that if I told him I would be admitting to all the lies I'd told him about my previous experiences.

Molly and I remained attached for a while, which was to my benefit as I had no experience whatsoever. In the evenings we would go to Da Mario, a shabby Italian restaurant off Queens Gate, and eat carbonara, which she would pay for, and then I would stay at her flat.

After a few months, I took Molly to meet Dad. He was sitting alone in his music room with tears running down his face.

'He's gone, Bax ... Pete's gone.'

I knew immediately what he meant.

Strangler had come back to England without telling anyone and he'd driven straight to Bournemouth to see his mum. He was found looking over the wall of his old school by the local police, who all knew him well. He was arrested on several outstanding warrants. They took him back to the station and let him sleep with the cell door open. In the morning he was found dead. There was no coroner's report or clear explanation for his death but it was assumed it was a heart attack. Maybe he knew he was going to die and that's why he came back home.

Dad and I sobbed for the whole evening, reminiscing about everything funny, good and bad about Strangler. We always knew that it was going to happen at some point but it was a horrible shock when it did.

Strangler's funeral was uncharacteristically sedate,

unlike his predictions of a glass coffin with Lemmy doing lines of speed off the top of it. It took place in a sleepy suburb of Bournemouth with a handful of ancient relatives and a small contingent from London. Ben, Toby, Zenaide and I drove down with Molly in her car. Dad followed in his new green Ford Granada with Micky at the wheel wearing a chauffeur's hat. En route we stopped at a small, anonymous pub on the side of an A-road. Dad had arranged to meet a man, who he later told me had just escaped from an open prison to attend Strangler's funeral. He handed over a shopping bag containing his HMS prison uniform as a gift to Dad.

We all sat in the back of a tiny church while a priest recounted a version of Strangler's life. He spoke of his wonderful contribution to the community and his strength of faith. It was strangely unsettling to hear the rhetoric of God applied to him. Marge, Strangler's mum, nodded her head enthusiastically throughout the ceremony, and was comforted by several family members. She then stood up and spoke honestly about her son. She said that not everyone understood him as that's the way he wanted it but when you were chosen to be liked by him then you totally got him. He was, among all his flaws, committed to the people he liked and that's what defined him.

It was an intimate gathering that didn't measure up to the crazy glory of Strangler's way of life. Instead it conveyed the simple truth that he wasn't immortal.

On the way back we got stuck in traffic on the M4 and Dad, now a little drunk, told Micky to gently ram the back of Molly's car. All I could see through the wing mirror on the passenger side was Micky, still wearing his chauffeur's cap and disgruntled expression, and Dad's cheeky grin.

14

COMMUNICATION
BREAKDOWN

Soho, London, 1990

After finishing her A levels, Molly went to the
Chelsea School of Art to do a foundation course
and moved into a shared flat in Parsons Green. I
hovered around her and we continued, in a flexible
way, to date. Lottie, her flatmate, hated me as she
felt I was a burden on their fragile student economy,
and I most likely was. A few mishaps had occurred
along the way in my relationship with Molly, and

I, being the less experienced person in everything except chaos, suffered the most. But we remained a couple under the constant threat of collapse. This tested the patience of everyone around us, especially Lottie.

Molly and Lottie decided to rent out the front room to reduce their costs and found Josh. He was a little older than us and had been educated at Harrow School, and was now working as an estate agent. He was short with a choirboy haircut and bad clothes.

After a few months we found Josh sleeping naked on the sofa, and a pungent aroma permeating the front room. This was when we realised he was smoking heroin at night. This transpired to be quite the norm among his peer group from Harrow, a boarding school full of entitlement. Josh and I slowly became friendly, mostly so I could defend myself against Lottie, who I was scared of. I had no real reason to be effectively living at the flat, and as usual had no money and no occupation.

Josh was full of convoluted entrepreneurial ideas that had no real hope of fruition but he was quite persuasive. I suggested we should start a nightclub and he immediately agreed, and we set out a plan to raise the funds.

The following week he quit his job and we spent our time working out the logistics of our new enterprise. Once we had the idea nailed, Josh knew exactly which banks we should approach and how much money we should realistically ask for.

Within two weeks we had a meeting with the business manager at NatWest on Chiswick High Road, which conveniently was my bank, and applied for a £2000 loan. We presented our vague plan, the costings for a year and a made-up business name.

Within a week the loan was approved with extortionate interest rates. We invested in two pagers, the pre-mobile phone devices exclusive to doctors and drug dealers, that allowed contact via primitive texts. We then bought two ounces of hash, which we planned to sell to Molly's art-student friends. This would provide a small income while we set up the business.

We squabbled about everything from the club name to the style of the flyer. We commissioned various artist to help design a logo and eventually, after briefly calling it Hazy Days, settled on Prime Time.

With high ambitions, we scoured the West End

for suitable venues that could hold over a thousand people and found Shaftesbury's on Shaftesbury Avenue in the heart of Soho. It was owned by a large Scottish ex-doorman who had every intention of taking everything he could squeeze out of us. So, after a few inept negotiations, we settled on hiring the club on a Thursday night for the handsome sum of £1000, half of our budget, and we wouldn't get any proceeds from the bar.

The night of the opening was a great success, mostly for the owner of Shaftsbury's, who made us count out the thousand pounds before the evening was complete. Seb Fontaine, who would go on to be a resident DJ at Cream, DJed and all my friends came in for free so we made a very small amount on the door. Josh and I were totally bankrupt within twenty minutes of the doors opening.

Not long afterwards, I was invited to Molly's family mansion in Lincolnshire, to meet her stepfather, Patty. Molly, her mum and I sat at an enormous dining table with Patty at one end. Patty was elderly with a forebidding Churchillian presence. He had one wooden leg, from a hunting accident, which he tapped on the floor, creating extra tension. After dinner Molly and her mum excused themselves so Patty and I could talk, which was a combination of polite inconsequential witter and an interview. He asked me what I thought about stuff and what I wanted to do with my life. His face remained unimpressed throughout and we made zero connection, not surprisingly as I was awkward and unwashed. Molly showed me the family's E-Type Jaguar and then took me round the grounds on a golf buggy.

Prime Time was never repeated and our aspiration to become nightclub proprietors was abandoned. The large debt accrued huge amounts of interest until the bank wrote it off.

Molly and I struggled through the next year but eventually she was signed up by Premier models and sent to Japan for six months, which marked the completion of our efforts. The next time I saw her she was posted across the underwear section of every Marks & Spencer store. I found this hard to reconcile with but, painfully, I always made sure to walk past her.

Hammersmith, London, 1991

I went back to live at Dad's briefly as Mum had now moved to Wales to look after Lilian, her mum, since my grandfather had passed away.

Dad was now seeing Elaine, who was the producer of a TV programme he briefly worked on as presenter. *Metro*, as it was known, was a late-night arts and culture show but was cancelled after being badly reviewed, not helped by an incident in which Dad spat at an opera singer during a performance he was forced to review.

Elaine tried her hardest to understand Dad's unpredictable side and celebrate the more positive moments but he constantly let her down.

Irene was an old friend of Dad's who would show up from time to time and they would smoke weed and listen to music. One afternoon after they had consumed a bottle of rum, Dad badgered me to get him some more. I went to the local off-licence and, as I was returning, noticed Elaine parking her car at the end of the road.

When I entered the flat both Dad and Irene were no longer in the music room where I'd left them and his bedroom door was closed. I embarrassingly knocked on the door and said, 'Elaine's here, Dad.' There was no reply and so I banged again. 'DAD, ELAINE IS HERE.'

'Open my fucking door then,' he said.

Which was the last thing I wanted to do. As I twisted the handle the mechanism disintegrated and the long metal shaft with the handle at one end came away, leaving the door sealed.

Then the doorbell rang.

'Just answer the door, man,' he said and chuckled.

So I did.

Elaine walked in and I smiled manically at her. We both went into the front room and she stood with her back to the balcony doors.

She asked where Dad was and I continued smiling. Behind her, I could see Irene's head bobbing up and down as she attempted to climb out of Dad's bedroom window on to the balcony. Once safe, she started to wave at me and I instinctively waved back and said, 'You know Irene, don't you, Elaine?'

Then I proceeded to slide the outside layer of double glazing back and undo the various locks on the balcony doors. 'Hey, Irene, you know Elaine, don't you?'

'Not really sure,' Irene said without much concern for maintaining the facade.

At this very moment Dad started to scream, 'Kick my fucking door in,' and then laughed madly.

Elaine had been silent for a while, trying to piece together a shape of all the bizarre goings-on.

I eventually broke the lock and found Dad standing on the other side in a red dressing gown with a big sinister grin. I knew then that, for my own sanity, I couldn't stay with him for much longer.

Barcelona, 1992

So I went to live in Barcelona. By then I was twenty. I'd been invited to stay with Lola, who was an old family friend of Zenaide's mum. She encouraged a few of us to come out and teach English. Spain was undergoing a major transition, seventeen years after the death of General Franco and a few years after it had joined what was just about to become the European Union. The Olympics had just been in Barcelona and the whole place had been transformed into a modern city, but the infrastructure of old Spain still existed and it was still very cheap to live there.

Lola was kindly but openly honest. When she felt it was necessary, she didn't cushion her words. She had the faint trace of Welsh left in her pan-European accent. Her relentless work ethic had saved her from the lifestyle perils that had ruined lots of her generation who had enjoyed the sixties and seventies to the fullest. Her background was shrouded in mystery and unsubstantiated rumours. Apparently she had escaped from prison a few years before arriving in Spain but this was hard to clarify. I knew that she raised her two children, Grace and Marlon, in Guatemala and hadn't been back to England for years.

I'd met her briefly while visiting Zenaide and she had immediately spotted something in me that, in her view, needed saving. In the same way, she had seen something in Zenaide but had fared better with him as I was a different level of dysfunctional. Zenaide had the foundation of an education and glowed with Latin appeal.

A few years after establishing herself in Barcelona, she moved on from teaching English to translating legal documents from several European languages into Spanish. She could write and speak French, German, Italian, English, Spanish and, most importantly, Catalan.

Her apartment was in the then rundown area of Gràcia in the middle of the city. It was a compact space with just enough room to accommodate herself, Carlos and now me. Carlos was tall and handsome with tiny dreadlocks. He was a classical guitar virtuoso trying to get to America to complete his studies at the Juilliard conservatory. He had escaped from Cuba only a month before, after disappearing from the concert he was invited to play at in Madrid. Carlos was exceptionally paranoid about being arrested by the Cuban secret police who apparently were hidden everywhere in the city. As a result, he never left the apartment and just sat in the room next to mine playing complicated musical scales all day and night.

When I arrived, the first thing Lola noticed was that the sole of my shoe was hanging off and it made an irritating flapping noise, which gave her some indication of what she was dealing with. She took the shoe off me and glued it back together. The first couple of weeks were fun as it was September and still quite hot, the Paralympics were on and the city was in festive spirits. I visited every English school I could find to drop off my CV, which was mostly fictionalised.

Lola's daughter-in-law Veronica – Marlon's wife – who was studying law, taught me Spanish once a week to give me some basic understanding of grammar in both Spanish and English.

After three weeks it was obvious that I was not going to find employment as an English teacher. I had zero understanding of how to conjugate a verb and, no matter how desperately fraudulent most of the schools were, I was beyond their limits.

This led to the first openly tense moment I had with Lola, who hadn't realised how incapable I was. She did not disguise her disappointment, and bluntly told me that I needed to find a job immediately.

It was very apparent I couldn't cook either. Carlos began to take pity on me as he could see that I hadn't eaten properly for weeks. He would share bits of his simple food and then, out of frustration, began to teach me the basics of Cuban cooking. We would make rice with salsa sauce and boiled eggs and, if we could afford it, some cheap sausage.

My sole employment opportunity came in the form of Lucho. He was a bucktoothed Peruvian man of a small stature who intermittently dated Lola. Everything about Lucho suggested corruption, from his greasy, slicked-back hair and sleeveless black T-shirts to his horrible smile. He ran a decorating business that served the wealthier Barcelonans. They mostly lived on the other side of Tibidabo, a mountain that overlooked the north-west of the city. He would pick me up early in the morning and I would sit in the back of his truck with a German man who would usually refuse to speak English, even though I knew he was fluent.

Lucho couldn't speak any English either and communicated with a series of frustrated facial expressions. He would repeat over and over again in Spanish the colour we needed to paint. 'Azul, azul, azul.'

We started work on a gigantic finca on the other side of the mountain. I had the task of whitewashing the walls and cleaning all the brushes. Neither Lucho nor the German would ever speak to me unless the German wanted to say something critical about the English. After a week, Lucho took me to a bathroom. He spoke to me intensely using his hands to illustrate what he wanted me to do. He pointed at one wall and said, 'Azul, azul,' and then at the other wall, with a newly fitted bath and a sleek designer sink, and said, 'Aquí nada más que aquí amarillo.'

He repeated this so many times that I eventually just agreed with him. Then he and the German went for lunch, leaving me with some tins of blue and yellow paint.

I painted one of the walls yellow and the other blue. When Lucho came back I suspected I may have made a mistake when he started shouting at me. He kept saying 'No el maldito azul,' over and over again.

At this point the German decided to intervene. 'Man, Lucho's pissed. You really got to sort this shit out.'

Lucho drove off in his van. I spent the next three hours trying to whitewash my initial mistake. Finally I stood on the sleek sink trying to reach the last corner. The whole sink came away from the wall and the pipe burst, and water jetted out everywhere. The German arrived and just stared in satisfaction at my demise. Lucho never paid me for any of the work I had done.

This put me in a critical situation and I had no idea how I was going to survive. I didn't even have a ticket home. I had successfully made no money in two months.

A few nights later Lola woke me up early in the

morning and said she needed to speak to me. We sat in the bar at the end of the street.

At first she commented that I was, to put it mildly, a mess but she said I was likeable and that may save me eventually.

She asked me bluntly, 'What the fuck did your parents do with you? Were you never asked to do anything around the house?'

She then asked if I was curious why she lived in Barcelona and how she'd got there. She said she knew there were rumours about her and then proceeded to tell me her story while chain-smoking Ducados, a Spanish brand of filterless cigarettes.

It began in the early 1970s in Ladbroke Grove, where her husband at the time was a heroin dealer. When she flushed his stash down the toilet in protest at his lifestyle, he beat her up. A month later she ran away to Guatemala, taking the kids with her. The country had been ravished by an ongoing civil war but it was a place where you could disappear, which is exactly what she did. She became romantically involved with a young rebel who was helping to lead a guerrilla movement fighting against the dictatorship. He encouraged her to smuggle cocaine into Europe and America to raise funds for their cause. For the next ten years she was a successful drug mule, never once being stopped until she got caught coming into London in the late seventies. She spent years in different jails, and was at one point extradited to the United States. Finally, she ended up in a high-security prison in Switzerland. One day, after seven years in confinement, she was placed into a laundry basket, put in the back of a van, dropped off at the side of a motorway and set free. She moved from one safe house to another around Europe before entering Spain, which at the time was a much easier country to hide in.

Once a week, she would ask Carlos and me to leave the apartment while a lawyer would update her on her current Interpol status. She never revealed why she was helped to escape or why she hadn't been caught since, but suggested she just knew too much.

The story blew my mind and I couldn't sleep that night. It felt like the whole apartment was bulging with fugitives, although pathetically the only thing I was trying to escape from was myself. I suddenly had an overwhelming need to get home. But how?

The next day I attempted to get my hair cut using the last of my pesetas and the little Spanish I'd learned. The barber shaved the side of my head and left the top long, which made me look like I was from a Steinbeck novel.

Two days later, I set off for home. All I had was a ferry ticket from Calais to Dover. I had to somehow get myself to Paris. I bunked some trains and eventually made it to the Gare de l'Est, where I managed to steal a cup of coffee and a croissant.

When I did finally arrive home I felt strangely empowered by my experience. Lola had a scary determination to survive, no matter the odds, and that left an impression on me.

15

ANNEKA, MARCUS AND MUM

Newport and Alicante, 1993–5

After I came back from Barcelona I managed to get a job working on a TV programme called *Challenge Anneka* as a production assistant. The premise of the show centred on its host Anneka Rice as she attempted to complete a series of challenges that aided communities. For instance, she would rebuild a homeless shelter in a week or set up a charity helpline for children. A brightly coloured beach buggy with Anneka at the wheel would leap out of the back of a huge truck, signifying the start of the timed challenge. She wore a neon-blue jumpsuit with splashes of pink and a red hard hat that made her appear both capable and exciting. Most of the work involved was completed behind the scenes by a collection of skilled professionals. Anneka would be filmed tapping in the last tile. Each programme was edited to create a sense of mounting tension that the task would not be finished by the deadline.

I was asked to get my driving licence as quickly as possible as the production team wanted to drive to Croatia in a UN-assisted convoy to help rebuild a school after it had been destroyed in the Balkan conflict. I was excited at the prospect and honoured that they had asked me.

Peggy, my granny, had suffered a stroke and was put into an old people's home close to where she lived in Hampstead. Dad moved into her flat so he could visit her every day and tried to look after her dog, Lucky. The staff loved Dad as he would entertain the other residents by calling out the bingo numbers or telling them lewd stories. The last time I saw Granny she winked at me and said, 'Stanley, this war won't last forever and then it will be different for us. Now take down some notes,' and she gave me a pen and some paper. I imagine she was reliving an episode when Stanley was her secret love interest, which may explain why she never did get back with Bill, my grandad.

Dad and Sophy had been seeing each other for a year and were now expecting a baby, so she moved into the Hampstead flat as well. This gave Dad new vigour and focus.

I stayed in Hammersmith on my own but the boiler had broken down and Dad refused to get it fixed. This was a ploy to slowly force me out. I had to boil several kettles just to make a shallow bath and the nights were freezing, but I wasn't paying any rent.

I decided to go and stay with Mum, who was now permanently living in Newport in Wales, so I could learn to get away from all the distractions of London and the cold conditions of Hammersmith.

Mum and Clive picked me up from the station and drove to a supermarket to collect some food for that evening's dinner. While Clive went into the shop, Mum stayed in the back of the car for a chat. She told me she had been diagnosed with cancer and it was inoperable. She had been given only a year to live. I didn't say anything.

The following year was extremely tough. I never did pass my test or go to Croatia. After a few months of going back and forth to Wales, Jemima came and stayed with Mum to look after her with Clive.

Meanwhile, Dad was offered the part of De Flores in a filmed modernisation of Thomas Middleton's *The Changeling*. The caveat was that his payment would be deferred until the film had made its money back, which appeared unlikely. Marcus Thompson, the director, had already put up his family home as collateral. Dad decided to commit to the project on the basis he could bring anyone with him, and he probably wanted the adventure. The first six weeks of filming would take place around the actual Santa Barbara castle in the centre of Alicante, the original setting for the Jacobean play. Marcus had secured several villas on the outskirts of the town and had personally persuaded a cast and crew to join the unpaid venture. John Cooper Clarke, Vivian Stanshall and Billy Connolly were among the cast. Amanda Ray-King, the leading lady, had begun an affair with Marcus, who subsequently left his wife. Even before the first day of filming the entire situation was a farce and a potential tinderbox.

Dad suggested that I come and help him settle in for the first few days of filming. I would accompany Smart Mart, one of Dad's trusted friends, who would be responsible for most of the duties. For me, it was just a short distraction away from home in Newport.

We arrived in Alicante and were picked up by Marcus and Keith, the first assistant director. Marcus was wearing a pale white double-denim ensemble with a terrible pair of cowboy boots and a ubiquitous director's cap. His long hair and apologetic demeanour hinted at the unforeseen dangers that lay ahead. Keith was a combination of twitches and smiles. He had war weary eyes, and was wearing a bandana and a sleeveless combat shirt.

We drove out of Alicante, past the Puig Campana mountain, and arrived at a very remote villa an hour later. Marcus gave a motivational speech about how wonderful this project was going to be before abandoning us without any food or means of getting any.

The next morning we were picked up and driven to the castle to meet the rest of the cast and crew.

Marcus had persuaded Eduardo, Alicante's chief of police, to cooperate in helping with the film. For the first few weeks we had special parking dispensations anywhere we wanted, within reason, and usually a couple of police outriders accompanied us everywhere.

A bedraggled collection of techs, make-up artists, actors and other mercenaries gathered around Keith as he explained the plan for the next week's filming. Riki Butland, the director of photography, was a giant with a displeased face. He sounded like a south London gangster. His cameraman Dave had the faded look of the past and possibly liked a drink. He was barely able to stand up straight without the assistance of a tripod or a sturdy piece of equipment.

Everyone there had a reason to accept not being paid. Either they considered this an opportunity to move up in the ranks of the film world or they needed to escape from something back home – it was like joining the Foreign Legion. There was a perfect mix of wannabes, try hards and criminals.

Dad lapped up every second of the ensuing chaos. He loved the cronyism created by Riki and his select bubble of men. It was very quickly clear that Marcus had a very adaptable plan, which lent an exciting uncertainty to each day.

I was only meant to be there for a couple of days but it had already been a week. I made friends with the younger members of the crew and moved over to where they were staying in an apartment block that overlooked the sea in a tiny town outside Alicante.

Within two weeks of filming the strain was starting to show on Keith, who was displaying increasingly erratic behaviour. The budget needed to feed a crew of thirty people didn't seem to have featured in the original planning. There was also the logistical nightmare of looking after a large group marooned in a collection of remote villas.

After an argument with Marcus and Riki, Keith went AWOL. For two days, filming carried on quite smoothly with one of the younger crew members taking over.

After dinner one evening Marcus, Riki and his friend Pete the Receipt, who had come over to help bail out the production, were leaving when Keith launched himself at their car. He was bare-chested and his eyes were on fire. It looked like he'd painted mud on his face. Keith had been living out on the side of the road for a few days, and this situation had pushed him over the edge.

The next day he apologised and was never seen again.

Between all the drama, I flew back home to visit Mum for a few days. Jemima and Clive had found a routine in caring for her and she appeared frail but very peaceful. It was strange to be back in the stillness of Wales. I longed to be in Alicante where the madness and the extremes helped mask the sadness of the situation back home.

When I arrived back in Spain a few days later, I discovered I had been promoted to third assistant director. This would normally be a meteoric rise but these were desperate circumstances.

George, like a lot of the crew, was from the pop-video world and *Middleton's Changeling*, as the film was titled, gave him the opportunity to become a second assistant director. He and I became insep-arable as we had a shared instinct to seek out as much trouble as possible, which I needed more than anything at that point.

We had a tendency just to disappear and not be seen for a few days. Maria, who was suppos-edly Spanish royalty and had a tenuous role as a location scout, was more interested in showing us the wilder side of Alicante. After being lost for two days we found ourselves stuck in the town without any money or means of getting back to our accommodation.

Drunkenly we called Eduardo, the chief of police, who arranged for us to be driven back in one of his squad cars. We pretended there was a camera crew hidden in the mountains and, if the cop permitted, they would film the car driving with the sirens flashing. He obliged us but I could sense he knew we were taking the piss. We sat in the back of the police car, trying to hide our hysterics. George started eating a huge lump of hash to see how far we could push our luck, and small bits of it were stuck to his teeth.

The next day, the police turned on everyone. They stopped us filming in the street, they randomly searched some of the crew, and no one showed up on motorbikes to give us an escort.

Everything gradually got worse and crazier from that point on as tiredness, hunger and bad inter-crew relations complicated proceedings.

Dad relocated to the very top of the thirty-storey Gran Sol Hotel, a monstrous seventies skyscraper in Alicante, and remained mischievously drunk for the final few weeks.

Towards the end of the filming schedule – nearly six weeks of madness – Vivian Stanshall, once of the Bonzo Dog Doo-Dah Band, arrived to play his small part. He was frail and being looked after by a young helper who acted as his nurse. The infrastructure of the production had disappeared by this stage and there was no clear instruction on what he had to do. A few days later, he went missing. Everyone frantically searched for him, desperately worried about his fate. Eventually George and I found him lying star-shaped and face down in the foyer of the Gran Sol Hotel. He was unconscious. He'd escaped from his carer and gone on a drinking frenzy for the first time in years.

The more insane it got, the more I enjoyed it as it felt further way from the impending truth I had to face when I got home. The last thing I remember was Alicante's fire fiesta or, as it was known, the Bonfires of Saint John. The locals threw fireworks at each other while wearing grotesque masks. Through our tiredness we revelled in how surreal and medieval it felt and danced and drank until the early hours. I lay down in the middle of the street and fell asleep surrounded by fire and people walking over me. I was woken up by a policeman kicking me in the ribs in the morning.

The filming carried on for a while longer in London as Marcus had somehow managed to acquire a disused car park next to the Cubby Broccoli sound stage at Pinewood Studios. A few of my new friends from the crew came and stayed with me in the Hammersmith flat and the madness continued for another few weeks. I'd purposely buried myself so deeply in the making of *Middleton's Changeling* I'd almost managed to forget that Mum was dying. But I knew I had to get back to Wales to see her.

She was now permanently in hospital and less coherent. It had been nearly a year since her diagnosis and it felt like she didn't have much time left. She spoke about seeing tunnels and old friends as she went in and out of consciousness.

One morning, I was told to come to the hospital. It was the very last moment before she went. She suddenly switched off and that was it. I left the hospital and walked around Newport, a town of sometimes unflattering greyness. I phoned Zenaide and we both cried. I was twenty-two years old and Mum was only fifty-two.

A few months after Mum died, Peggy, my granny, passed away. I can barely remember that happening

because of the loss of Mum. Dad was totally dev-
astated but, unbelievably, two weeks after that, on
2 January 1995, my brother Bill was born and life
continued.

ACKNOWLEDGEMENTS

Thanks to Will Birch for his incredible research for *Ian Dury: The Definitive Biography*. To my sister Jemima Dury. To my very oldest friend Ajmal Jay Sadiq. To Felix and Ferdie. To Little Chris and Spider. To Micky and Ben Gallagher. To Ben Campbell-White and Zenaide Martinoli. Huge thanks to James Oldham at Rough Trade Management for pushing this forward. To Jeannette Lee, also at Rough Trade Management, for being so supportive. A huge thanks to James Gurbutt and Olivia Hutchings at Little, Brown for allowing me to do this and babysitting the process. And lastly to Howard Watson who brilliantly copy-edited this book and kept it close to its chaotic spirit.